BRAVE NEW MOM

Jessie Everts, PhD, LMFT

A Survival Guide
for Mindfully
Navigating
POSTPARTUM
MOTHERHOOD

ISBN 13: 978-1-63489-429-6

Library of Congress Catalog Number has been applied for.
Printed in the United States of America
First Printing: 2021

25   24   23   22   21   5   4   3   2   1

Cover design by Emily Mahon
Interior design by Cindy Samargia Laun

Wise Ink Creative Publishing
807 Broadway St. NE, Suite 46
Minneapolis, MN 55413
wiseink.com

BEING A MOM CAN BE MAGICAL.
The feeling of your new baby sleeping
in your arms. The first little smile or
laugh. The tremendous feeling of love that
washes over you. It can be beautiful and
miraculous and full and awe-inspiring
and humbling and blessed and a privilege.

It can be heavy too.

Mothers aren't "supposed" to talk about the other feelings: the darkness, loneliness, judgment, lack of appreciation, exhaustion, and lack of self. Many feel depressed and anxious. The weight and importance of "motherhood" can feel overwhelming, even dangerous and terrifying. At best, motherhood is a lot of responsibility. At worst, it can feel like a life sentence.

This book is for the mom who is up in the middle of the night feeding her child, lacking sleep, not sure how much longer she can take it. This book is for the mama who is terrified that something will happen to her or to her child. Hold on. This is for the mother who is scared of what she will do. We see you.

I want you and all the moms to know that you're not alone, that what you're feeling is okay, and that there is a way through. In my therapy practice, I've seen every kind of mom there is, like the very well-off mom who looks like she has it all together but under the surface is feeling depressed and anxious, with a constant pit in her stomach. I've seen the new mom who is homeless, living in her car with her baby and trying to do the best she can while feeling ashamed to ask for help. I've seen the many, many moms who are in survival mode and feel like they're drowning but can't even spare a minute to think about how they're feeling. And I've been there too—with all these fancy degrees but not a clue what to do when my colicky baby just. keeps. crying.

I see you. I've seen you in my therapy office, not even sure what to ask for because it seems so desperate and impossible. I've been you, at home alone with your baby and thinking, Who in the world thought it was a good idea to leave me home alone with a baby? And I have read about you in research studies and therapy guides that talk about how it can get better. I want to bring those resources to you, so you have them when you need them, in the middle of the night or in the middle of what feels like an ocean where you're treading water, keeping your head barely above the surface. We're here. Hold on.

TABLE OF CONTENTS

WELCOME TO THE CLUB

Before you start this book, I want to welcome you into two things. First, I welcome you to the Club. Anyone who is reading this, has ever read this, or *will* ever read this is now part of this group of mothers, mamas, moms— or whatever you want to be called! This is the Club for mothers who can't remember the last time they got a good night of sleep. The Club is for mamas who stress about every little thing about their babies. It's also for mamas who are stressed and don't really know why. The Club is for moms who can't face another crying fit, another diaper change, another night of worry. And the mamas who love their babies so much they want to cry. We are all sisters through time who have faced this amazing, terrifying, and beautiful thing called motherhood (or mamahood, matriarchy, parenthood, or whatever you want to call it!). So WELCOME. You are one of us. We are all of us.

Second, I want to welcome you to a first practice, a bit of mindfulness to get you started and to put you in the mindset for this book. One of the hardest things about being a new mom is that you're very often in "survival mode" and not in the moment or taking time for yourself. This book is full of practices—because if you're not used to purposefully and consciously being in the moment or taking time out to self-reflect, you'll need to practice! There is no need to feel like you "should" be good at this right away. It takes practice to get better at something, and each little bit of practice is a little gift in and of itself.

So, I'd like to welcome you to practice an attitude of openness and acceptance. The first step to any of the work toward feeling better about yourself as a mom is to *accept yourself*. Yes, with the dirty hair, in your pajamas, covered in spit-up. You made a *person*. You are amazing. Practice acceptance toward your feelings, your doubts, your fears, and your joys. They are all *you*, and you are pretty powerful. When you think about what you are going through, I hope that you will *practice* feeling acceptance of yourself and open to being and feeling whatever you are in the moment. Be open to whatever comes. Take whatever benefits you, and know that it is more than okay. You are more than okay.

PRACTICE: *Starting with Openness and Acceptance*

1. Close your eyes for a moment and call to mind a feeling of openness and acceptance.

2. Take a few deep breaths and let them fill and open your heart.

3. Focus just on the feeling of openness and acceptance for a few breaths, then try to extend that feeling toward yourself, your journey, and your reality of this moment.

4. Whatever you are feeling, extend a feeling of openness and acceptance toward it.

5. Breathe in acceptance and a feeling of openness for yourself for a few moments.

One mom I know, Bria, became one by surprise (unplanned) in her early twenties. She loved her new baby so much, and realized that she was holding a lot of doubts about her ability to be a "good mom" to this tiny creature. Bria hadn't had a great relationship with her own mother, so she didn't have a model of the kind of mother that she wanted to be. Without a clear guide, Bria thought she didn't have any "maternal instincts" and felt like she did everything wrong. It took a lot of practice of trusting that she knew herself and her baby best, and that she did in fact know how to take good care of her new little family. Building a feeling of trust in herself started with being open and accepting of herself as a mother, with both strengths and weaknesses. Bria learned to trust and believe that she didn't have to have everything figured out to be a mom. She could just be the caring and loving mom she already was and be okay with not having all the answers.

Practicing being in a place of openness and acceptance helps you take in what might be helpful from this book and leave what isn't for you, without judgment or harsh feelings toward yourself or others. We are all on this journey, and we all need different things as we go. You may read this book ten times and get something different out of it each time. You will get something different from it than your best friend will. I want you to take in what is helpful for you in the place and time in which you're reading this book, so that you can get the most benefit from it and honor your own experience of motherhood.

Also, all names and identifying details about the moms whose important stories have contributed to this book have been changed to protect their privacy and confidentiality.

SOME NOTES ABOUT THIS BOOK

I wrote this book largely during the COVID-19 pandemic in 2020, when I was in "quarantine" with my family. It was a hard time that also reminded me of another difficult period in my life, when I had my two babies and was on maternity leave each time. I was an overachiever, and those were lonely and frustrating times for me because there were very few marks of "success" in the earliest days of motherhood. No one told me I was doing fine and that I was going to make it. Actually, I'm sure there were people who told me that. But I was living in survival mode, not really taking anything in. I was just trying to make it through each day.

I wrote this book as the guide I wish I had during that time, because I desperately wanted to live in the here and now and not miss the beautiful early moments with my babies, but didn't know how. This is my hope for you, reader and new parent out there: that you'll find ways to appreciate yourself for this amazing thing you have done. Maybe you'll practice dropping the judgment or comparisons that make you feel like you're not doing it well enough. And maybe you'll find the actual joy in it . . . sometimes.

I know that this book is limited in some important ways. For the sake of simplicity, I will refer to *mothers* or *moms* fairly often. I do not mean to exclude anyone who doesn't use these particular terms for their early parenthood. I want people who read this book to know that their perspectives are valid and maybe different from the dominant culture. Ideally, we would all have a book written specifically for each of us! So take anything from this book that applies to you and feels helpful, and please forgive any terms that might feel exclusive or that don't fit your experiences.

The same will be true for any circumstances that might not be specifically captured by the language used in this book. Often I will refer to your singular *baby*, though I recognize you may have had more than one. (And if you are a mom or parent of multiples, I see you and live in awe of you!) It wasn't possible to write *baby/babies* everywhere I wanted to, but know that I thought about you every time I referenced a *baby*.

Also, adoption, birth trauma, and babies with special needs or different abilities and requiring additional care are not specifically represented in this book. Please know that all of these complicated situations were on my mind while I was writing this book. I wish it had been possible to add all of the extra support and love that you need when things don't go as planned or if babyhood is not what you expected.

Finally, I recognize that, as a white woman, my experience of motherhood is far different and more privileged than that of many parents out there. Because of my own ongoing journey in recognizing and working to dismantle white supremacy—the fact that the white experience is taken for granted as the default or standard of value of experience—this was all on my mind as I wrote this book. I value so deeply the differences that show up in other cultures around motherhood, parenthood, and attachment; and I tried to bring that into this book as much as possible through examples and experiences other than the white experience that is still seen as dominant in America and beyond. I've done my best to immerse myself in others' experiences of new motherhood so that what is reflected in this book is not just my own, but rather many mothers' feelings of it. I honor and love everyone's differences; and this book is designed to offer critical resources, perspectives, and support to mothers from many different backgrounds.

I have such reverence for parents who have particularly unique or unrecognized challenges with their pregnancy, birth, and newborn phases of life. Please know that I thought of you while I was writing this book, and that while I wish I could have written it to fit every experience exactly, it just wasn't possible. I apologize for any exclusion, and I hope there will be something that makes you feel seen and supported in the writing that follows.

1

Reclaiming
Your Power:

From
"What Have I Done?"
to
**"I Have Done
Something AMAZING"**

FIRST OF ALL, PLEASE KNOW that I see the enormity of what has just happened to you. Your body has done this incredible thing. You have grown a human being inside you. If there are moments when you let yourself think about it, I hope you can allow yourself to marvel at the amazing feats that you are capable of.

The changes your body goes through during pregnancy and postpartum (i.e., after birth) are just miraculous. During pregnancy, changes affect every single organ system in your body. Blood volume and heart output (effort) both increase. Your metabolic rate increases by about 15 percent, and you use 20 percent more oxygen. Your glands work harder, your joints become looser, and your bones lose some density. Increasing hormone levels often make you nauseous. Your body is working hard to create a new equilibrium that you and your baby need.[1]

After birth, everything in your body is physically trying to go back to "normal" as quickly as possible. First of all, your body is fatigued from the physical exertion and pain you went through during birth. Your heart rate has to re-normalize, and your body gets rid of some of the excess tissue and fluid it was holding to support your baby. Your organs, especially your uterus and placental site, contract immediately to prevent any more blood loss. As soon as your baby is out, your body starts to try to remember what things were like when you were just one person. However, your breasts engorge and your mammary organs start to produce milk.[2] So while you're recovering from the physical trauma of giving birth, your body is automatically taking on more physical changes to sustain the life you just brought into the world.

If you think objectively about what your body has done, you can admire that it's an astonishing series of events! It's very common for women to feel dissatisfied with their bodies after giving birth.[3] When you miss your pre-baby body, or wish your stomach looked smoother, or that the weight would come off, gently remind yourself of the enormous and incredible transformations your body has accomplished. You created and grew life within you, and then birthed it out. YOU did that!

The magnitude of giving birth isn't just about how amazing your body is. It's also about the seismic shift in your life that comes with bringing a whole new person into it. There are monumental changes in your identity as a

reclaiming your power

15

person, the way you prioritize things, your role in your family, your time and attention, and your relationships. Almost everything changes when you have a baby. It's important to recognize how dramatic this shift really is, because a lot of the feelings of overwhelm that come with parenthood are really about these big-picture changes.

Unless you have some friends who have gone through this journey very recently (so they can remember it through the new-mom fog), no one really tells you how hard early motherhood is. Your feelings are all over the place, you don't know how to take care of this new and very vulnerable little person, and you don't have a lot of guidance through every decision and choice that has to be made to keep everyone alive and sane. But guess what? *You're not alone in feeling overwhelmed by this!* According to research, 75 percent of new moms said they weren't given enough guidance about the postpartum phase, and two-thirds said they found the postpartum phase more difficult than they expected. The same study found that 90 percent of new moms think that more education and guidance is needed.[4] So I hope that this book will help a little bit with understanding that what you're going through is *normal* and *hard*, and *it's going to be okay.*

For simplicity's sake, though, let's start with the physical feats of giving birth that just happened to you and how they can affect your well-being and mood.

YOUR BODY IS AMAZING

Starting with pregnancy, your body handled a lot. The first thing that happened when you became pregnant was a sudden and dramatic increase in the amounts of estrogen and progesterone your body produced. This created a lot of the growing environment for your baby as well as a lot of the side effects that weren't as much fun to experience. Estrogen helped your body create nutrient pathways for your baby by creating blood vessels in the uterus and placenta and supporting growth and development for your fetus. The increased estrogen also caused the nausea you probably experienced in your first trimester and the breast enlargement (due to milk duct development) during the second. Your amazing body produced more estrogen during one pregnancy than it will during the entire rest of your life!

Progesterone is the other major pregnancy hormone. It helped your body and organs such as your uterus stretch far beyond normal size to accommodate that baby. Progesterone also caused your ligaments and joints to loosen, all to make room and adjust to the impending weight gain, fluid retention, swelling, and shifting of your center of gravity. Amazingly, your body knew exactly how to do all of this without anyone telling it to.

The changing hormone levels also affected your mood, as you may have heard. The experience of the "baby blues" is so common in the first few weeks after giving birth that it's almost assumed that mothers will go through it.[5] That doesn't make it any easier, though. The baby blues—a period of time when you might have mood swings, irritability, tearfulness, confusion, and fatigue within the first ten days after giving birth (peaking around Day Five)—affects up to 85 percent of women who give birth,[6] and is directly linked to the drop in hormone levels that happens as soon as baby exits your body. Some women are more sensitive to the changes to their progesterone or stress-related hormone levels, which can make us feel especially irritable, weepy, or emotional after giving birth.[7] These mood shifts are a sign of how significant the birth experience is for you and your body, and can be a reminder to treat yourself with extra kindness. Remember, you have been through some things!

Also common but more serious is postpartum depression, or *PPD*, which affects somewhere between 10 and 20 percent of mothers, and one in ten partners.[8,9] Postpartum anxiety is also a concern, affecting about one in ten mothers.[10] These are longer-lasting periods of symptoms of depression or worry/anxiety that may need to be treated by a mental health professional or therapist. These conditions will be discussed later in this book, because you'll want to be aware of the risk factors and plans of action in case a mental health issue arises after giving birth that you can't handle on your own.

Understanding that your mood is being influenced by these chemical shifts and is not within your control can help with thoughts like, *Is there something wrong with me?* No, there's not, though you might feel that way at times. This is new territory for your body and your emotions.

It can be hard to appreciate the amazing changes that happened to your body during pregnancy and birth. Often our bodies feel irreversibly changed by these experiences, and we might feel negatively toward our post-baby bodies. This is understandable, and it can be helpful to practice conscious gratitude toward your body so that you can maintain a positive and compassionate feeling toward yourself during this physical and emotional transition time.

PRACTICE: *Honoring Your Body's Changes*

Dedicate 5–10 minutes for this practice.

Lie down somewhere quiet, and start to breathe deeply and relax. Then slowly scan up your body, starting with your feet and going up to your head, and reflect on each part of you. When your thoughts wander, gently bring them back to the part of your body you're scanning. At each part, reflect and honor yourself for the changes that have happened since having a baby. These changes aren't good or bad; they are amazing, and they are okay. Think about how amazing and strong each part of your body really is.

When you find yourself feeling judgmental about any part of your body, set that judgment aside for the moment and focus on recognizing and revering each part of your body—not for what it looks like or how it feels at that moment, but for what it can do. Bring your mind to the beauty and amazingness of each part of you, just for this time.

Write about your experience. How did it feel to do this body scan and practice appreciation for your body?

_____

_____

_____

_____

_____

_____

_____

_____

Even though there might be things you wished were different about your body, try this practice every day until you can start to feel some appreciation toward your amazing body for growing a baby and for enabling you to do all of the things you can do for yourself and others. This body is yours for life! It will feel better to love it than to hate it.

YOUR LIFE IS CHANGING IN AMAZING WAYS

It would be one thing if the physical changes happened all by themselves. But there is another emotionally complicated part of going through a pregnancy: coming out of it with a baby to take home and a whole new role in life as a mother. This is what the science world calls "a pivotal and paradoxical life event."[11] To most of us, this feels like a totally unprecedented shift. Even if you felt well prepared for motherhood throughout your pregnancy, Day One at home with your baby can feel overwhelming.

One mom I knew was totally shocked when they told her she could leave the hospital with her new baby. Of course, she had known this was going to happen, but so much of her attention throughout her pregnancy was on the birth plan that she hadn't thought about going home and what comes next. A single parent by choice, she had loved ones set up to drive her home and visit her when she arrived. But when, inevitably, everyone left and she was home alone with her new baby, she felt panicked and unsure of what to do. "I just sat there and stared at my sleeping baby for what felt like hours," she recalled. "I didn't know what to do, and this home that I loved suddenly felt like a scary and lonely place." It felt like her whole life had changed in that couple of days she had been away in the hospital.

Having a baby can change the meaning of your life. It certainly changes the focus of life, since you spend the first days figuring out what your baby needs and when. This doesn't allow for much thinking about your existence as a whole separate person—in fact, you might feel as if you have lost your sense of self altogether. You might go days without thinking about showering or making yourself a meal. Since you're thrown into a new life that is focused on baby's every cry and need and that prioritizes your physical recovery from giving birth and the baby's medical milestones like ounces of weight gained, it's hard to capture something as immeasurable as the total shift in your life's purpose and the thoughts and feelings that come along with it.

When you feel overwhelmed or sad about these new expectations, practicing kindness and acceptance can be comforting. It's okay to feel sad or regretful about how your life has changed after having a baby. You can use those feelings to help you recognize the magnitude of what has happened in your life. Any big change comes with mixed feelings of excitement or anxiousness. Letting go of old ways is bittersweet. Rather than denying or avoiding your feelings, accept the monumental impact this has left on you and your world.

PRACTICE: *Reflecting on Your Experience*

Reflect on your birth and your new parent experience so far. Take a moment to feel the enormity of what has happened and how your life has changed. Write down whatever feels important about your experience of pregnancy, giving birth, and being a new parent. Let yourself feel amazed and proud of what you have gone through.

Most importantly, you experienced these changes in ways that were unique to you. Everyone's pregnancy and birth experience is different. Many factors affect how you may feel about your birth experience: your age, whether your pregnancy was planned or not, the amount of social support you feel like you have, the medical interventions that happened during delivery, cultural beliefs about birth and delivery, the amount of control you feel you have in the delivery or birth planning, and any fear you have going into the birth experience.[12] All of these factors are so unique to you that there is no single birth story—and the *meaning* of having a baby and expanding your family is also incredibly special and distinctive.

There may be times when it's more important to connect with other mothers or parents than it is to have had the same exact experience. This goes back to the practice of openness and acceptance from the introduction. You can be open to connecting with someone who had a different experience than you, yet find things that you share and that make you feel validated and seen.

PRACTICE: *Exploring Your Birth Story and Recovery*

Write about the changes you experienced in your body when you were pregnant. What came at the beginning? What happened later?

Did you notice any changes in your mood? What did you notice? When did it happen?

How have you felt about your recovery from the birth experience? What would you like to feel better about?

What are your goals for yourself, your baby, and/or your family over the next few months? Instead of setting goals that depend on certain milestones, what goals could you set that you would enjoy or that would enhance how you'd like to feel?

SURVIVAL MODE

A common experience for new moms is the feeling that they spend most of their time in "survival mode." In other words, they feel like they're just getting by and aren't able to stop and think or make thoughtful choices or decisions. One mom I know described this as the "getting-through-the-day." She recognized so many little things to think, care, and worry about with her new baby. She felt there was no room to enjoy, reflect, or do anything for herself. All of her energy was spent on simply getting through the day.

This survival mode is really a sensation of increased overall stress. Our bodies and brains are existing in a heightened state. Physically, it's our nervous system's "fight-or-flight" response operating constantly to keep us feeling a little bit on edge. The fight-or-flight response is supposed to be engaged when there is a threat to our survival or a danger to us that we need to respond to quickly.[13] Because all of your protective instincts are active in a new heightened state with a tiny, defenseless baby in your care, your brain mistakenly releases the same stress hormones that you need to be alert during a real emergency.

Living in survival mode takes a toll on your mental and physical well-being because rest, calm, peace, and the present moment are all on hold. If you recognize that you're in survival mode, though, you can practice stepping outside of it when you need to. You "need to" when you notice that you haven't taken a deep breath all day because you've been so focused on your baby, or if you haven't had time to think about or appreciate anything that's happening. Survival mode takes you out of the present moment and puts you into autopilot or numbness about what you're doing so that we can *just do it*. If you live in that survival mode all the time, you can start to be numb to things you don't want to miss, such as beautiful interactions with your baby or with your partner or actual enjoyment in the life you're living. You don't want to miss this stuff. So you might need to learn how to press pause on survival mode to make sure you're really, fully *in* your life, at least once in a while.

PRACTICE: *Taking a Moment Out of Survival Mode*

If you notice that you're in survival mode—meaning that you haven't taken a deep breath, a real moment of rest, or a completely present and unstressed second in your day—then it's time for you to pause.

Take a deep breath in, hold it, then exhale it completely. Hold for a few seconds with your air exhaled all the way out. You might count in for five counts, out for five or more counts, and then hold for two counts. Repeat this five times in a row (or ten, if you're really feeling stressed).

As you do this as many times as you need, clear your mind of thoughts about anything other than this deep breathing. Focus on how it feels to inhale your lungs full of air, hold, and exhale out all of your air, and feeling the pause.

That pause is incredibly important. It's a powerful way of resetting your nervous system, taking a moment to get out of your stress or fight-or-flight response, and truly letting your body and brain rest in the present moment.

Repeat this deep breathing and clearing of your mind as long as you need to, and as many times a day as you notice that you're in survival mode and need to check back in with yourself and reset.

Having a baby today is different than it ever has been. Many women are delaying having a baby until they're established in their careers or enter a committed relationship. As a result, the average age of first motherhood, or the age when a woman gives birth for the first time, has climbed from the early twenties in 1980 to the late twenties in 2018[14] and is continuing to trend upward from there. Women who are becoming new mothers are older, more established or settled in their lives, and also arguably more isolated.[15] Fertility rates have declined,[16] and more women are having babies on their own, either outside of a relationship or as single mothers (by choice or not), than ever before.[17] The history and interplay of factors that have led to all of these things is complex, but what it leaves us with is that many new moms are coming into motherhood with more struggles, more time and attention demands than ever before, and less help and support.

For all of these reasons, we feel more stress in our roles as mothers than many before us have.[18] Instead of letting this stress weigh us down or continuing to just *survive* through early motherhood, it becomes even more important for us to take care of ourselves, think purposefully about finding support from others, be realistic about our difficulties, and find ways to express and deal with our feelings. *That* is what this book is about.

SELF-CARE FOR NEW MOMS

Taking purposeful care of ourselves as new mothers is often far down on the list of priorities. But it is *vitally important* to our ongoing mental health and our relationships with our baby and our support people. A study of new moms in the 1990s found that, six months after having a baby, over 80 percent of the moms hadn't resumed the self-care activities that they identified were helpful for their mental health and wellness.[19] If you're neglecting to take care of yourself, you won't be at your best to take care of anyone else.[20] If you only take one thing away from this book, I hope that you learn to pay attention to your own self and offer it more regular care and nurturing.

Self-care is the practice of noticing and taking care of your own emotional and physical needs. While that may sound simple, it gets a lot more complicated for a parent of a new baby. First, your attention is almost always needed for baby-related things. Second, many of us don't have a lot of experience with taking the time to think about what we feel and need or what boosts our mood.

This is what makes self-care a *practice*: it has to be done consciously and consistently so that we learn how to do it and get better at it, just like learning to drive a car. We're not all naturally good at it, but we can be if we put conscious effort into making it a priority. The first element to making self-care a practice is to find the time to do it. While it's true that babies require a lot of time and attention, it isn't true that they require *all* of your time and attention *all* of the time. I know it feels like they do. But the stakes are high for you to carve out a little time for yourself. A study found that not feeling able to practice self-care was significantly correlated with postpartum depression.[21]

Other studies have shown that self-care is an important part of a mom's well-being and that mothers often see selflessness as the goal in motherhood.[22,23] Somehow we see being a mother as synonymous with giving up our own needs and feelings to be solely and wholly devoted to caring for our children. This dangerous societal message comes at the cost of women's well-being when they become mothers. This message also contributes to our sense of being overwhelmed, unseen, and underappreciated. Our well-being depends on not disappearing into motherhood but instead, as Chimamanda Ngozi Adichie says, on being "a full person."[24] We can be mothers, love our children, and still be whole people in our own right. In fact, we are better at all of it if we do maintain our sense of self, our identity, and a recognition of our feelings, needs, and hopes.

Research shows that self-care is one of seven areas of attention that mothers *need* in order to function at our best. The others are social support, psychological well-being, infant care, interaction with your baby, management, and adjustment.[25] All of these will be defined and discussed throughout this book. The important thing for you to know up front is this: *Mothers need to pay attention to themselves so that they can be there for their babies!*

Self-care has to be done through conscious effort because it's a skill. We improve through practice. Taking time each day to focus a little bit on ourselves builds up our reservoirs of positive energy, which we absolutely need if we're sharing our energy with our baby, our partner or family, and anyone else who might need it.

You don't need to carve out hours of time for self-care. Start with ten or twenty minutes a day, even if it's broken into a few different chunks between baby care and trying to sleep. You may need to put this in your schedule or planner as dedicated time so that you can protect it and remind yourself to spend time focusing on yourself and something that would feel good to you. This is important time—as important as anything else you'll do during the day—so treat it as such. Don't let other tasks take priority, and don't put it off until you're so stressed that it becomes more like emergency care than regular, consistent care of your body, emotions, mind, and self.

Because our emotions are tied to our physical health, lots of self-care practices are about movement, getting outside, creating good habits around sleep and nutrition, and otherwise caring for our bodies. After all, our bodies have been through a lot recently! Other self-care practices focus on taking care of your mind and emotions. Spending some time alone or in nature or doing an activity that's soothing to you—such as listening to music, taking a long bath or shower, journaling, gardening, or going to therapy—serve to center you and boost your levels of calm and happiness. If that isn't vital to a new mom, I don't know what is.

reclaiming your power

Self-care doesn't have to be rigorous or take a lot of time. Start with things that are gentle and nurturing to your spirit, even if it's just two minutes of deep breathing. Here are some ideas to get you started:

PRACTICE: *Building in Self-Care*

Choose one self-care activity to practice today.

Take Some Alone Time: Ask someone else to care for baby for a bit, or use some of the time when your baby is sleeping or occupied to give yourself a break and do something just for you.

Move Your Body: Walk, jog, hike, bike, do strength-building or yoga—anything that moves your body and makes you feel strong.

Cuddle with Your Baby: Without thinking about other things, enjoy a few moments of cuddling and being with your baby in a close and comforting way—for both of you!

Do Deep Breathing: Practice the exercise on page 24, even if you're not feeling stressed. Taking deep, full breaths settles your body and helps you keep a calmer baseline.

Cooking/Baking: If you enjoy being creative in the kitchen, spend some time cooking or baking, and pay attention to your senses (i.e., what you smell, see, feel, hear, and taste).

Spend Time in Nature: The links between nature and mental health are clear.[26,27] Being out in the "wild" (or just in your yard) can make you feel happier. Take a walk or take your baby to a park or nature preserve nearby. Feel connected to the earth and all of its beautiful sights and sounds.

Listen to Music: Playing music (even in the background) as you do everyday tasks can lighten your mood and make you feel soothed and comforted.

Take a Long Bath or Shower: Water is very soothing, so give yourself extra time to enjoy the warmth and feel of water around you.

Try a Yoga Video: Even gentle yoga can get you in touch with the present moment and your body, giving your mind a rest from all of the other things that might be going on.

Dance with or Sing to Your Baby: Small moments of connection strengthen the bond between you and your baby. They can also lift your mood! Even smiling at your baby, whether you feel like it or not, releases endorphins that can trick your mind into feeling happier.[28]

Meditate: Taking a few moments to close your eyes, bring your mind to your breath or to the present moment, and clear out extra or distracting thoughts can help you develop a calmness within you that you can return to when you need it.

Learn about or Practice a Cultural Ritual: Grounding yourself in cultural practices—either your own or someone else's—can focus your attention on something meaningful and interconnecting. This can be a specific kind of prayer, music, art creation, storytelling, or something that has deep roots and connections to others and to ancestors.

Garden: Getting into the dirt is another way to bring your focus to body sensations and a purpose. It's also a practice in hope, by planting and caring for something now that will bear fruit (or flower) later, and a way to show care for your self and your world.

Sleep is an essential part of self-care. I know that practicing good "sleep hygiene" might not feel possible as a new mom. If your baby has a hard time falling asleep or wakes frequently throughout the night, you probably experience the kind of sleep deprivation that is so common for new moms and can be so incredibly hard to deal with.

Here are a few elements of sleep hygiene to practice even if your baby doesn't sleep well. Introduce the ones that feel most possible for you.

PRACTICE: *Attending to Sleep*

Choose any of the elements of good sleep hygiene below that feel achievable to you, and incorporate them into your day:

- Go to bed only when you feel sleepy. If you force yourself to sleep when you're not feeling tired, you'll just get frustrated with yourself.

- Avoid doing any activity other than sleeping or sex in your bedroom. That way, the room is associated with sleep in your mind.

- Maintain as regular a sleep schedule as you can by going to bed at the same time each night and/or waking up at the same time each morning.

- Exercise more than three hours before you plan to go to bed to allow your body and mind to relax and calm down.

- Avoid alcohol, nicotine, and other stimulants.

- Avoid caffeine for at least six hours before you plan to go to bed.

- Reduce light and noise in your bedroom as much as you can.

- Avoid using electronic media right before trying to sleep. Instead, do something that you find relaxing such as reading, journaling, or listening to music or meditations.

- If you can't fall asleep, or if you wake and have a hard time getting back to sleep after being awake for thirty minutes, get out of bed and go to another room to do something soothing or calming. Go back to bed when you feel sleepy, and try again.

My first baby didn't sleep more than two or three hours at a time until she was well over a year old, and I felt personally victimized by the lack of sleep I got during that time. I didn't think there was anything I could do. Yet looking back, I realized I was caught in a cycle of frustration about my sleep that caused me more stress and immobilized me from trying *anything* to improve it. The actual lack of sleep was debilitating, but my resentment and frustration were what kept me awake.

There are many parts of new motherhood that we can't control—how much our baby sleeps or doesn't, when we need to feed them, when we need to bathe them, how to keep them happy. Self-care is about taking time to focus on the things we *can* control, like how we spend our time. We can fixate on what is overwhelming, or we can focus on things that make us feel happy and peaceful. Whichever place we put our attention is likely to grow.

HONORING YOUR SELF AND YOUR JOURNEY

Think about it for a minute: you are really quite strong, and you have accomplished amazing things! One amazing thing about you is that you have *made it* this far—in life, and in this book. That means you have some amazing strengths that carry you through hard times, and an ability to hold on even when you don't feel like you have any strength left. A lot can be said about the strength and endurance of mothers. We each go through tremendous challenges and a hundred daily hardships, yet we carry on— sometimes without any recognition or appreciation at all. It's up to us, then, to recognize and appreciate ourselves for the things we can handle.

More hard things will come. When we live through the first year of having a new baby, we're rewarded with the rest of their and our lives of motherhood, with increasingly complicated parenting decisions and issues. So we need to keep in mind that we are on a long journey here, and there is no reward for getting to the end in the best shape or having gotten the most sleep. The reward is the relationships that we build with our children, our families, and—maybe most important—*ourselves* along the way.

PRACTICE: *Giving Appreciation, Love, and Gratitude for Your Self and Your Journey*

Take a moment to recognize all of the things you've gone through that have helped you get to where you are today.

Give yourself some appreciation, love, and gratitude for the hard things you've been through that have made you the strong person you are today.

Consider where in your body you feel strong. When you think about your strength, where is it? It may be near your heart or in your legs, shoulders, or back. What does strength feel like for you, in your body?

Take a few minutes to reflect on the feeling you identified. See if, by paying attention to it, you can amplify it a little. Feel your strength grow just a bit.

Locating and feeling the strength that you have can help you remember that strength is within you all along your journey.

Wherever you are on your new mom journey, it's wonderful that you are here. I want you, me, and everyone who reads this book to lower that statistic of 80 percent of new moms who don't take care of themselves.[29] It is a travesty that so many new moms think they are not on their own list of priorities, and that kind of neglect makes us feel emotionally bad on top of being mentally and physically exhausted. I hope that the practices in this book will help you understand and accept what you're feeling, check in with and take care of yourself during this difficult time, and maybe even enjoy this time and your baby.

INTRODUCTION & CHAPTER 1 CHECKLIST

*Here are the practices
you learned in this chapter:*

1. Starting with Openness and Acceptance
2. Honoring Your Body's Changes
3. Reflecting on Your Experience
4. Exploring Your Birth Story and Recovery
5. Taking a Moment Out of Survival Mode
6. Building in Self-Care
7. Attending to Sleep
8. Giving Appreciation, Love, and Gratitude for
   Your Self and Your Journey

Pick two favorites from the list above. Write them on a piece of paper and tape it to your bathroom mirror. Make the practices that were useful to you a part of your daily routine, and consider marking the ones that were harder to connect with so you can explore them further or try them again later. Practice doesn't make perfect, but it helps to make it a habit and deepen the positive effects the more you try these exercises.

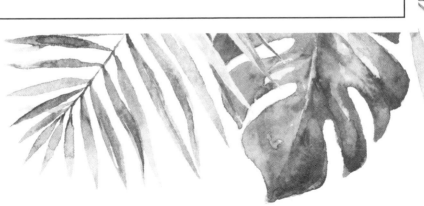

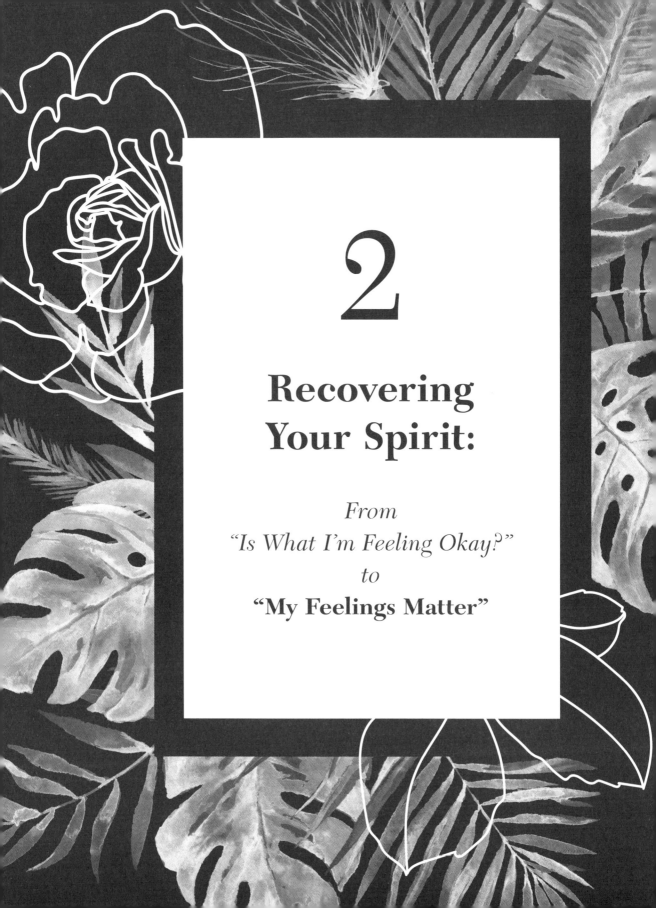

2

Recovering Your Spirit:

From
"Is What I'm Feeling Okay?"
to
"My Feelings Matter"

AFTER HAVING HER FIRST CHILD, Sadie described herself as "crazy" and "a basketcase." Her mood was all over the map, scary thoughts about her baby were always popping into her head, and she felt like her personality had changed overnight. She worried her partner would hate her because of it, so she didn't let them know how she was feeling. For months, she sat at home, feeling like there was something wrong with her, and not wanting anyone to know. She realized she needed to open up when her partner kindly said, "You're so good with the baby," and Sadie burst into tears.

You have a lot of feelings. We all do! Having a baby amplifies all the feelings you already had and adds a whole range of new ones related to this new role you have in life as well as changes in your identity, your body, relationships, responsibilities, time, focus, and the list goes on. Your feelings might take enter stage for the first time in your life. Some of us are used to shutting down emotions, coping with them in unhealthy ways, or pretending they aren't important. Having a baby and physically needing to be at home and resting gives you lots of time to think about how you feel. And how you feel is often pretty out of control.

Start by understanding that there are reasons (often physical or physiological) for your feelings. They exist for a reason and aren't in and of themselves "good" or "bad" or otherwise. They are FINE. They just *are*! If you recognize that there are reasons for the emotions you're experiencing, you can allow them to happen without trying to stop or stifle them—because if you bottle them up, they'll leak out in unexpected ways.

The hormones that flooded you when you were pregnant are one of the culprits of all of these wild, out-of-control emotions. Those high levels of estrogen and progesterone from pregnancy plummet as soon as you give birth. This is one of the reasons why an estimated 80 percent of women experience the baby blues in the first few days after giving birth. Your hormone levels take a dramatic dive all at once as soon as baby is born.[1,2]

The baby blues can include the following symptoms:

- Feeling weepy or crying for no apparent reason
- Impatience or irritability
- Feelings of sadness
- Restlessness
- Feeling fatigued or overly tired
- Trouble sleeping, even when you might be able to (i.e., when baby is sleeping)
- Mood changes
- Poor concentration
- Anxiety or an unusually high level of worry[3]

The baby blues usually resolves itself within two weeks. If you have some of these issues longer than two weeks, it might be related to sleep deprivation, physical recovery from birth, and/or the enormity of the change that has happened in your life. However, if your experience with any of the above symptoms feels dangerous, lasts longer, or gets in the way of your ability to function and connect with your baby, it may indicate postpartum depression or anxiety, which may require working with a therapist. These issues will be discussed further in chapter 4.

Whatever the case, be open with your partner, support people, and your doctor about how you're feeling after giving birth. Dealing with new and scary feelings by yourself may reinforce your feelings of isolation and might start you down a path that gets harder and harder to escape from when you need help. If you're worried about your postpartum moods or symptoms, mention it to someone you trust and be open to their response. If they suggest talking to a doctor or therapist, think about it. It may also feel better to have let someone know how you're really doing.

MOM FEELINGS ARE COMPLICATED

Of course, the baby blues aren't the only feelings you might be having. And it might not be quite as simple as just the hormone levels. Your mood after having a baby is also complicated by all of the major life changes that happen concurrently. It's normal to feel grief or sadness about the loss of freedom or identity that comes with having a baby.[4] Many of us assumed or were told that having a baby would be the happiest time in our lives. It might be hard to allow ourselves to have other feelings about it too. The truth is, having a baby is a very complex emotional time in our lives; and it's absolutely okay to recognize you have feelings of sadness, loss, self-doubt, exhaustion, worry, and loneliness as well as extreme love, joy, and maybe a deep connection that you've never felt before.

Look at the emotions wheel below. It shows how interrelated and overlapping all of the different feelings are. Think about how some feelings are a combination of the basic feelings of happiness, fear, anger, and sadness. Surprise, which might be thought of as the overlap of happy and fearful, can range from being excited or energized to feeling shocked or dismayed—a very different experience of being surprised about something. Often what we show on the outside isn't representative of how we feel on the inside. We might show up as angry or irritated, but what we feel inside is inadequate or overwhelmed. It can be helpful to know that feelings are complex and often all jumbled up together, which can lead to us acting in ways that we might not love or that might not reflect how we really feel.

PRACTICE: *Identifying Your Feelings*

Think about a time when you acted in a way you didn't like or later regretted. Identify on the feelings wheel what kind of behavior you showed or how someone else may have viewed you. Then find the true feelings on the wheel. Notice the distance between how you acted and how you felt, as well as whether you have discomfort showing feelings in a certain area of the wheel. Consider how you could show these feelings more accurately or genuinely, and practice this with someone you trust.

Relationship changes may also weigh heavily on you after having a baby. If you have a partner, it's likely that both your attention and theirs are mostly on the baby, which is a big change from when it was just the two of you. Often there are small—or big—areas of disagreement or differences in understanding about parenting, what should be done and by whom. It's impossible to work out all of these details before the baby arrives because you just don't know all of the things that will come up during the eventful first year of parenthood. Maybe your partner has a different idea about what to do when the baby wakes up at night than you do. You may feel resentful about how little support and help you get from your partner, and you may feel bad about your body or the lack of intimacy in your relationship. The first year of parenting is a hard time for a couple because each of you are dealing with insecurity about your ability to parent as well as the changes to your relationship dynamics.

Research from the Gottman Institute on relationships shows that 67 percent of couples experience a decline in their satisfaction with their relationship in the first few years after their first baby is born.[5] Having a baby is a trying and difficult adjustment for a relationship. What the research shows is that having or developing a deep friendship with your partner helps you to stay connected—or to reconnect—after having a baby.

You're creating a *new* partner relationship as parents during this time. Instead of focusing on how things used to be between you, consider how you'd like your parenting/partner relationship to look going forward. It can be helpful to think about the two of you as a team in parenting. Otherwise, you'll often feel at odds or as if there are more frustrations than positive moments. To be on the same team, you'll need to express your feelings and frustrations and come up with solutions together—rather than holding everything in and hoping your partner can read your mind.

We'll talk more about getting support from your partner in chapter 3. But if feeling disconnected is a stressful area for your relationship in this new parent stage, start with a simple practice.

PRACTICE: *Engaging Mindfully with Your Partner*

Once a day, spend a few minutes checking in with your partner about how each of you are feeling. Put your phones away, and focus on each other for these few minutes. Listen as fully as you can, and don't worry about offering solutions. Just listen with the intention to hear and communicate understanding and support. Make sure you each take a turn and then appreciate each other, creating a sense that you're on the same team and in solidarity with each other.

If you're a single parent, you might have the same issues of disagreement or misunderstanding with your support people. Or you might feel alone in your questions and decision-making, which can feel scary. Being a single parent is harder for so many reasons, none of which have to do with your abilities as a parent. For the most part, if you're a single parent, you have fewer resources available to help you with parenting than two-parent families: less time, less money, and less physical and emotional energy. Even though all of those things aren't within your control, it's incredibly common for single parents to feel guilty about how much they can be with or provide for their children.

This is a complicated form of *mom guilt*, which is so, so common and will be discussed later in this book. For now, it may be helpful to notice when you experience guilt as a parent (single or otherwise) and unhinge it from your actions so you don't end up "guilt parenting," or acting toward your children based on guilty feelings.

PRACTICE: *Separating Yourself from Guilt*

Notice how guilt comes into your life as a parent. You might feel guilty about not being with your baby as much as you wish you could be because of work, custody arrangements, or other reasons. You might feel guilty when you get frustrated or irritated about your role as a parent. Or you might feel guilty about needing or wanting time away from your baby. In whatever ways you experience guilt, think about the thought behind the feeling of guilt. Often the thought is something like, *I should want to be with them all the time.*

Recognize that "should" thoughts aren't helpful. They set a standard for you as a mom that might not be realistic or even applicable to your life. They are based in judgments that we might hear from society or other moms, not from real experience and acceptance of the way things really are.

When you find yourself having guilty "should" thoughts, change the thought to see whether the feelings also change. Take that *should* out of your brain's commentary. If you can replace it with something like, *I will feel better if I can . . .* , the rest of the sentence is bound to be more realistic and achievable—and you'll feel better telling it to yourself.

As you find a more realistic, less judgmental thought to practice, make sure to exhale that guilty feeling as much as you can. You're doing the best you can. Choose what to do out of that more supportive thinking, instead of out of the guilty thinking about what you "should" do.

FEELING ALL THE FEELINGS

Many of us aren't used to showing our feelings freely. Some of us aren't even used to *feeling* our feelings freely. This is a practice. Especially if you grew up in a family where feelings weren't a big topic of conversation, you probably don't have guidelines for which feelings are "normal" or what feelings are "supposed to" feel like. Allowing yourself to have your feelings, to experience them without shutting them down or stifling them, is a real skill that you might not have a lot of education about.

The practice starts with just observing what you're feeling. Language can sometimes get in the way with this practice, because we have such limited words for the different nuances of feeling and can't always adequately describe those nuances in words. Instead, start with the sensations you're feeling in your body: tightness or openness in your chest, tension or looseness in your shoulders or stomach, pressure or lightness in your forehead, and so on. Emotions are really how we interpret these body signals and what we think caused them.

PRACTICE: *Identifying Your Sensations and Feelings*

Sit quietly for a few moments, and focus on what feelings are going on inside you. You can start by thinking about the bodily sensations you notice.

Then identify the feeling that may be behind the sensations. You can start with basic emotions such as happiness, sadness, or anger. Sit with the feeling, whatever it may be, and be curious about it for a few moments. Write down what you notice:

Next is to practice nonjudgment toward your feelings. This may seem impossible or contradictory. Many of us live in constant judgment; we're always trying to figure out how things compare, like who "wore it better" and what we do and don't like. It's a natural instinct to judge all of the information that comes at you to first determine whether or not it is important to your life and survival, and then to decide what to do with it. Practicing nonjudgment means suspending these decisions and judgments for a while.

Judging ourselves and our feelings leads to trouble because it can feed or exacerbate negative feelings. Feeling lonely or resentful doesn't feel great, but we make it worse by telling ourselves that we shouldn't feel the way we feel, that it is bad, and that we need to stop feeling that way. There is an old saying that goes, "pain is inevitable; suffering is optional." We're all going to experience difficult feelings. But if we fight against those feelings instead of accepting them and moving forward from them, we suffer unnecessarily.

The same is true if we spend a lot of time on judgmental thoughts about ourselves, our abilities, and our bodies. It creates unnecessary and unhelpful suffering instead of appreciation and acceptance of the things we can't always change immediately. Think of it this way:

$$Pain + Acceptance = Pain$$
$$Pain + Nonacceptance = Suffering$$

Judging ourselves over something we're feeling and believing it is "bad" adds an extra layer of suffering. Now we feel bad about the fact that we feel a certain way. The alternative, letting go of that judgment toward ourselves and our feelings, allows us to have our feelings without beating ourselves up or focusing on what we *should* or *shouldn't* feel or be.

One study showed that the mindfulness component of "nonjudging of inner experience" (practicing nonjudgment toward your internal feelings and sensations) during pregnancy was highly correlated with maternal mental health, including less depression, anxiety, and stress.[6] The practice of recognizing and letting go of our judgmental thoughts, especially the ones that we direct toward ourselves, can make us feel more positive and accepting of what is going on, both for ourselves and for others.

PRACTICE: *Observing Your Feelings Nonjudgmentally*

When you're feeling upset, observe your feelings and see how you can be nonjudgmental toward yourself. Sit quietly and reflect on what sensations are going on within you, without trying to change or stop them. Just observe what is going on. If you find yourself slipping into judgment, gently remind yourself that your feelings are neither good nor bad; they are okay. Practice holding the feeling without judgment, and notice what happens to the feeling the longer you observe it.

It's important to note that practicing nonjudgment isn't the same as not having an opinion. You absolutely have a right to have an opinion about anything. But it may be helpful to consider how often your opinions are rooted in thinking that something is inherently *good* or *bad*, because thinking in these judgmental terms can inadvertently make you feel negatively toward yourself or others. If you notice that there is judgment in your opinions, determine where these judgments come from. Do they come from things you were taught or that you and your family took for granted when you were growing up? If this is the case, think about whether those are opinions (or judgments) that you *want* to continue to hold and if they continue to serve you. Sometimes they don't! For instance, if you grew up in a religious home where your family's belief was that homosexuality was a sin and "wrong," you might have absorbed this judgment without thinking more deeply about it.

recovering your spirit

45

One of the few joys of being an adult is that you get to examine these old automatic beliefs to see if they still fit or are helpful to you. If not, *you can change them!* Moreover, you can change your opinions when you receive new information. Considering how you think is important to making sure that you're being authentic in your thoughts and actions. That way, you're believing things that you truly believe, for reasons that are important to you.

It's absolutely okay to have opinions. Practicing nonjudgment is about examining any beliefs you have about what is right or wrong, or what is good or bad, and seeing how holding those judgments might cause you to react in ways that don't serve you. Observing things for what they are, without judgment, allows you to be more in touch with your thoughts and feelings and less reactive. It also helps you build trust in yourself that you can choose how to respond, rather than acting out of instinct or unexamined beliefs.

PREGNANCY AND LOSS

For a lot of us, having a baby isn't as straightforward as all of the pieces we just talked about. For many of us, there is a feeling of grief or loss that might be involved in having a baby. Maybe this is our first baby after suffering from a miscarriage or pregnancy loss. Maybe a family member died before or during the pregnancy, and now our memories of them are tied in with our postpartum feelings. Or maybe the loss of our previous lifestyle or sense of self is particularly hard to face.

Pregnancy loss—whether called miscarriage, stillbirth, fetal loss or death, or termination of pregnancy—is more common than we might think. Up to 15 percent of known pregnancies end in pregnancy loss, and the rates are probably much higher for women who don't know that they're pregnant. Some research estimates that 25 to 43 percent of women will experience a pregnancy loss at some time in their lives.[7] Pregnancy loss happens for a number of medical reasons; and no matter what the cause is, it's almost always an emotional and distressing time. Even women who choose to terminate a pregnancy can experience considerable grief and emotional distress that may be exacerbated by the thought that they "chose" this and "should be okay" with their decision.

If you had any significant loss during your pregnancy or after the birth of your child, recognize that you may be going through a grieving process on top of all of the emotional and hormonal changes that we already talked about. It's okay to feel sad after you've had a baby. It's even okay to feel sad about your baby. If your baby came at the same time as a big loss, you might not be able to look at your baby without also thinking about the loss.

One new mom I know, Anya, experienced medical complications during her first pregnancy. She delivered her baby several weeks early only to watch her baby live in the newborn intensive care unit (NICU) for over two months before passing away. Anya and her spouse experienced an enormous amount of grief. They had been waiting to have a baby for several years. After some time, Anya became pregnant again, and her anxiety was (understandably) extremely high throughout the pregnancy and the first year of her second baby's life because of the traumatic memories of her birth and postpartum experience with her first child.

For me, the whole experience of pregnancy, birth, and having a newborn baby was bittersweet because my mother passed away a few years before I had my first child. I didn't have her there so we could talk about my excitement or fears, compare my experiences to hers, or watch her become a grandmother. While it was a happy time for me and my partner, a piece of the joy was missing. I saw other women enjoying and deepening their relationships with their mothers but couldn't do the same with my own.

We have to lift some of the pressure off of ourselves to have only positive feelings about being pregnant and having a new baby. We also have to make sure we're lifting it off of other moms. Most mothers experience some negative feelings, like discomfort, frustration, fear, anxiety, lack of confidence, sadness. Those of us who also have feelings of loss or grief need to know that our pregnancy and motherhood experiences are no less real, valid, or impactful because of the complicated emotions that come with it. And we, as mothers, need to know—and make it known—that it is possible for this time in our journey to be both joyful and difficult.

PRACTICE: *Working through Feelings of Loss*

Think about your pregnancy, birth experience, and new motherhood as a journey—one that began long before you were pregnant and will extend throughout your whole life as a mother. Recognize the wide range of feelings you've had through this part of your journey. Consider how you may have experienced these feelings according to the *Five Stages of Grief* model, which was created by Elisabeth Kübler-Ross:

- **Denial:** Wishing it hadn't happened, trying not to think about it

- **Anger:** Blaming yourself or others, having punishing thoughts or guilt

- **Bargaining:** Thinking *what if*, wishing you could go back in time and change something

- **Depression:** Feeling deep sadness about the loss, recognizing the space it left in your life

- **Acceptance:** Coming to realize that you can't change what happened, finding some peace and starting to move forward

Know that these stages aren't experienced in a straight line but are woven throughout in an arc that becomes an important part of your story and your journey. When you experience these feelings, befriend them instead of pushing them away. Sit with them, and be gentle with them and with yourself. These feelings are natural, and they're not your enemies. Feeling them, instead of stifling them, is the only way to move through this process and continue on your journey.

Denial   *Anger*   *Bargaining*   *Depression*   *Acceptance*

HOW TO DEAL WITH THOSE COMPLEX FEELINGS

When your mood feels out of control, a few things can help. First, starting at the body level, take some deep, cleansing breaths and release them fully. This can help your parasympathetic nervous system to engage and calm you from the inside. When our mood changes quickly or we have a wave of anxiety or worry, sometimes our fight-or-flight response activates when it doesn't need to. Our protective instincts are hardwired to react quickly by bracing for a crisis, shutting down, or running away. Some people respond in this way more quickly because of past traumatic events, sensitivity, or anxiety. Practices like deep breathing help us counter this reaction by consciously calling our parasympathetic nervous system, the *rest-and-digest* response, into action to soothe and calm us.

PRACTICE: *Calming Yourself with Deep Breathing*

Whatever your mood may be at this moment, take a few seconds to practice some deep breathing.

Breathe in slowly for four counts, then release the breath for six counts. Pause at the end of your exhale, then do it again. Draw out or lengthen your count each time you repeat.

Start with five rounds of this deep breathing exercise.
Write about how you feel afterward:

Practice this once a day. The more you practice it when you aren't feeling agitated or anxious, the easier it will be to call on this skill when you do feel that you need it to help you calm down.

A second practice you may want to try when you're experiencing mood swings or worry targets the thought processes behind those moods or worries. For example, if your aunt visits and says something like, "What a beautiful baby. She looks so much like [insert your partner's name]," you might recoil if you think she is insulting you and she thinks your partner is better-looking. Your aunt might mean it this way, or she might not. Often our feelings are based on a thought or interpretation that may or may not be true or helpful. When something happens to us that creates an emotional reaction—say, if someone gives you parenting advice and you react in a resentful or angry way—the piece we often skim past is that how we interpreted what happened (i.e., what we thought about it) is the reason we experienced that feeling. If we interpret someone else's advice to mean that they think we're not a good parent or that they know our baby better than we do, it leads us to feel (and probably react) angry and resentful.

Slow down the process. Identify what is really happening. How are you interpreting things? Is your emotion based on what is actually happening? Or is it based on an assumption you've made? Is there a more helpful interpretation you can bring to this moment? Consciously identifying how you interpret a situation when you're reacting emotionally can help you diffuse the feeling and react in a more thoughtful way. For instance, imagine that your partner comments on how the house needs to be cleaned, and you flare up in anger. Take a step back and recognize that you may be interpreting your partner's words to mean that you're a bad housekeeper or that you should have time to clean. Then ask your partner if that's what they meant.

It's possible that your partner may have meant something different. Maybe they meant that the two of you should figure out how to divide up the house chores, because they know housekeeping isn't your first priority. Our emotional interpretation of things is often an assumption based on insecurity or something we feel especially sensitive about. We assume that the other person is aware of our sensitivity or is being intentionally critical or attacking when, in fact, they might not be. Finding a different interpretation or asking the other person what they meant may make us feel better. It may also provide an opportunity for us to respond more calmly.

Having just had a baby, we are especially sensitive and emotional, so we might make a lot more out of an off-hand comment than we'd normally intend. Connecting our feelings to the interpretation or thinking behind them can allow us to calm our feelings and maybe feel completely different.

PRACTICE: *Slowing Down Your Reaction*

When you have an emotional response, slow down the process of reacting right away. Take a moment to identify what you're feeling and what may have caused the feeling.

Think about how you interpreted the situation and how it may have led you to feel this way.

Is it possible you could interpret the situation differently? If so, how?

Consider how you can relax your interpretation or ask a question to see if it helps how you feel.

Research says that, in order to feel happier overall, we need to practice paying attention to good feelings as much as we might naturally be drawn toward negative feelings.[8] This means that we need to purposefully draw our attention to when we're feeling good, happy, and calm and prolong those feelings. Some may call this "savoring" the positive feelings.[9] If you don't love the word *savoring*, choose a different verb, like *enjoying, relishing, cherishing, appreciating,* or *treasuring.* The point is that you can expand positive feelings or make them more impactful or prevalent in your life by paying more attention to them and drawing them out as long as possible. This means that when you're having a quiet moment with your baby or enjoying some time to yourself, you can call your attention to the good feelings you're having, breathe them in, and really enjoy them so that you truly feel them and can recall those good feelings when things aren't going so smoothly and you aren't feeling so wonderful.

PRACTICE: *Savoring Positive Feelings*

The next time you're feeling good or positive, take a moment to feel those positive emotions and sensations in these ways:

- Breathe in and out, focusing on the feeling you're experiencing.
- Sit with the feeling for a little while longer than you usually would.
- Focus on enjoying the moment and the feeling of quiet and calm.

Congratulate yourself for building a skill in savoring positive emotions, and bring this positive feeling to mind at other times throughout your day.

A study published in the *American Journal of Orthopsychiatry* showed that new parents are typically most stressed about their perceptions of their own abilities or characteristics, such as mental and physical health, attachment or bonding abilities, sense of competence, changes to their roles in life, social isolation, and their relationship with their spouse.

Parents were less stressed about anything having to do with their baby—the baby's demandingness, adaptability, mood, recognition or interaction with the parent, or distractibility.[10] What this means is that we're often so in our own heads about parenting that we're more focused on what we think about how we're doing than on our baby!

To cope with feelings of inadequacy or self-doubt, do your best to get out of your head. Usually the only person who sees you as inadequate or incompetent as a parent is YOU! We're wired to be so tuned in to what we don't feel we do well that we think our flaws are glaringly obvious to everyone else. We also think that our perception is *true* when, in fact, our self-doubt might be a figment of our imagination. Instead of dwelling on thoughts about how poorly you're doing or how someone else is clearly doing this so much better than you, check out of your head and get involved in something else entirely.

PRACTICE: *Getting Out of Your Head*

When you notice that you're wallowing or feeling stuck in self-doubt, take a moment to recognize the thoughts you're having, then make a conscious shift to think about something more positive or to do something more productive. For example, shift your focus to the things you love about your baby or your partner. You could also go for a walk or do a chore you've been putting off. Put your full attention toward something else instead of dwelling on negative thoughts that aren't helpful and that might not be true.

The important thing to recognize is that fighting your feelings by stifling or denying them only causes you more suffering. It's easier, kinder, and better for your mental health to accept and feel your feelings, see them as an important part of you, and listen to them. Feelings are signals to ourselves, a sign to pay attention to something. This may mean being more fully present in the good moments of being a mother and being with your baby. It may also mean taking care of yourself when you're feeling discouraged or less confident in yourself.

CHAPTER 2 CHECKLIST

Here are the practices you learned in this chapter:

1. Identifying Your Feelings
2. Engaging Mindfully with Your Partner
3. Separating Yourself from Guilt
4. Identifying Your Sensations and Feelings
5. Observing Your Feelings Nonjudgmentally
6. Working Through Feelings of Loss
7. Calming Yourself with Deep Breathing
8. Slowing Down Your Reaction
9. Savoring Positive Feelings
10. Getting Out of Your Head

Pick two favorites from the list above. Write them on a piece of paper and tape it to your bathroom mirror. Make the practices that were useful to you a part of your daily routine, and consider marking the ones that were harder to connect with so you can explore them further or try them again later. Practice doesn't make perfect, but it helps to make it a habit and deepen the positive effects the more you try these exercises.

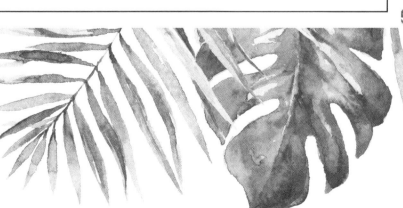

3

Embracing Your Community:

From
"I Feel Alone in This"
to
"I Am Worthy of
Love and Support"

*KAT DID A LOT TO PREPARE HERSELF for being
a single new mom. She had lots of connections and
close friends through her community and her church;
and she actively recruited them to be with her after
she gave birth, to bring her meals or to give her breaks
by babysitting. And then the COVID-19 pandemic hit.
Suddenly her team of helpers was unable to visit or
provide child care. Kat was alone with her baby with
very few outlets or supporters. She quickly realized that
she needed the social support desperately, no matter
if it needed to look different than she had planned.
She set up weekly video calls with several friends and
family members, asked people from church to drop off
groceries, and even asked neighbors to walk by and
wave or shout greetings to her and her baby each day.
Reminding herself that she had a team, though they
weren't as close or hands-on as she had hoped, buoyed
Kat's spirits and helped her realize how much her
friends and connections meant to her.*

Like a lot of new moms, you may be caught up in feelings of exhaustion, stress, and overwhelm; and you might not be focused on how much you deserve and need love and support during this time. You *do* deserve it. New parenthood is often an isolating time. Feeling on your own can compound your feelings of self-doubt or incompetence, so it's important to find and gather your support system during this time.

SOCIAL SUPPORT FOR POSTPARTUM MOMS

Having connections with others is essential in early motherhood for a number of reasons. First, it makes you feel less alone when you know personally that other moms who have gone through or are going through the same thing are out there. And knowing this is crucial! You need to know moms who have made it through this tough time and survived, despite how impossible it may have felt. You also need to know moms who are going through this right now, at the same time as you, and that you're all feeling similar things and experiencing similar struggles. When you're home with your baby most of the time, it can feel like it's just you who feels this way. That isn't true. Feeling support, care, and love from other mothers, parents, and even those who might not understand it personally but have the energy to show that they care—that's your lifeline, your buoy, your link to the outside world.

You might feel alone and isolated after giving birth. This can lead you to feel like all of your feelings and worries are unusual and unique, when really they are normal and shared among new moms and parents.[1] Talking with other parents about feelings and fears has a double benefit. It helps you realize that many parents share your experience. Second, it can build up your support network, which is important to your postpartum health, life satisfaction, well-being, and ability to deal with stress and mental health symptoms.[2,3,4,5,6,7]

It doesn't matter how many friends you have, or if you have a partner. The quality of your relationships matters more than the number of them. In fact, some research says that having *one* close, confiding relationship is most important to maternal mental health.[8]

Also, it matters more that you perceive you have support than whether you actually receive it. So take a moment to think about the army of mothers who have your back. There are millions of us! Think about all of the mothers out there cheering for you, wishing you well, knowing how hard it is, and holding on when you don't have the strength. Feel the power of that support. Relishing the feel of that support can buoy you when you need a lift.

Next, think about someone you know who does get it, and who wants the best for you. This can be someone in your life who supports you (even if it's from afar) or who you haven't talked to recently. Reach out to them. Share a little bit about what has been hard for you. Even if they didn't have the exact same hardship, they probably have had similar experiences or fears. Opening the door to extra support brings in a different perspective, which can be really important if you're stuck in your own thoughts. Another person's viewpoint can give you a little bit of hope and light.

PRACTICE: *Reaching Out*

Reach out to another parent you know. This person can be a new mom or someone of any age or stage of parenting. Ask them about their experience of being a new parent and if anything made them feel overwhelmed. Don't worry if their feelings or fears are different than yours. Instead, reflect on the similarities.

THE BENEFIT OF RELATIONSHIPS

Research has found specific reasons why we need relationships. R. Weiss showed that there are six main functions of our social relationships:

1. Guidance, or advice/information
2. Reliable alliance, or the ability to count on someone for assistance when we need it
3. Reassurance of our worth, or recognition by someone else of our competence, skills, and value
4. Attachment, or emotional closeness with another person that makes us feel secure
5. Social integration, or a feeling of shared interests, concerns, and connection
6. Nurturance, or the ability to rely on others to support our well-being[9]

Usually one of the six functions is foremost in each of our social relationships. Maybe we rely on our sister or mother for the emotional closeness of attachment and comfort, but we have another friend who is better for guidance or advice. But having a lot of support in one function doesn't make up for a lack of support in the other five. Ideally, we have one key relationship that serves many or all of the functions or a few relationships that cover them all.

PRACTICE: *Reflecting on Your Supports*

Reflect on the people in your life who are or could be considered part of your support system. Identify which ones fit each of these roles for you, knowing that one person can fit a few different categories:

1. Who gives good advice?
2. Who is reliable? Who is there for you when you need them?
3. Who is reassuring? Who makes you feel good about yourself?
4. Who do you feel closest to or most secure with?
5. Who do you have things in common with?
6. Who nurtures you? Who helps take care of you?

If you don't have a person for any category, think about how you could connect with someone in that specific way. For example, if you're lacking a person who gives good advice, consider whether a counselor, therapist, or parent educator might be helpful. If you don't have someone who shares your interests, consider whether you could join a group that would introduce you to new, like-minded people.

Take a moment to feel gratitude toward the people you identified. This is your support system! Recognize the important role they play in caring for you and helping you care for yourself (and your baby), especially during hard times.

It's okay if you feel you don't have a strong support system. The truth is, many new moms don't. If you're having babies earlier than, later than, or far away from your friends or family members, you might not have a natural support system in the listed functions. So if you know that you need more support than you have, don't give up on it. There are groups online and in your community that are created for the purpose of providing support to moms who might not already have it. When I was a new mom, I found online communities that were so helpful for my middle-of-the-night worries. When I was up at all hours feeding my daughter, I would think about what foods to introduce at what age or what questions to ask the pediatrician. And I'd always find answers out there in the online mom groups! At times, I would check in to see who was awake when I was and feel connected to other moms who were "in it" with me.

Also, completing the support system practice in this chapter may have made you aware of how you don't always look for these types of support from other people. Think about which types of support you look for frequently and which ones you don't. It might be that you like to be around a person who is reassuring, but you rarely ask for advice or actual help. Recognize that the areas where you don't reach out for support don't just go away. Consider whether you might be holding some judgment about getting certain kinds of support and how you can let go of those judgments so that you can feel more supported and strengthened. That's what support is, after all. It's a safety net or reinforcement—strength, not weakness.

PRACTICE: *Building Up Your Support System*

Here are some ways in which you can build up your support system:

Ask a friend to check in with you weekly, just to ask how you're doing and let you talk or vent a bit.

Reach out to one supportive person each day or week or as often as you need. It can be a different person each time, just to say hello or send some pictures of the baby. That way, you can make contact with someone outside of your own environment.

Go online and search for a *supportive* moms' group around a topic that you feel particularly stressed about, such as babies with special needs, NICU, postpartum depression, etc. *Supportive* is the key word here; some online mom groups can be pretty judgmental, and those are not the ones you want to go to for support.

Make a therapy appointment. This is what therapy is for: to have someone to talk to about how you're feeling. Many therapy clinics have telehealth options now, where you can meet with the therapist virtually. This makes it easier to talk to them, especially on the days you can't get out of the house (or your pajamas).

Create your own support group/team. Know that many moms out there are going through some of the same struggles as you and that they may also need help building their support systems. So reach out and create one yourself! Start by connecting with other moms in your area through Early Childhood Family Education (ECFE) or another parent group, then establish regular supportive meetings where you can connect as women and as moms.

ATTACHMENT: FEELING AND SHARING LOVE WITH YOUR BABY

Think for a minute about your beautiful, lovely, wonderful baby. It's okay if, in this moment, that's not how you feel. If your baby has been crying for an hour, won't eat, or won't go to sleep like you *know* they need to, you probably aren't thinking about your baby as beautiful and lovely right now. But when you can, consider how amazing and wonderful your baby is. Your baby certainly feels these things about you, even if they can't show it all the time. You and your baby are bonded in a unique and beautiful way. This bond is there through the delightful moments as well as—and maybe even more so—the difficult ones.

PRACTICE: *Seeing Yourself from Your Baby's Perspective*

You are your baby's whole world. Think about how much your baby loves you, and imagine what it must be like for your baby to receive your love and attention. Consider the ways in which you're positively providing for your baby. In what ways can you be even more present and positive with them today? Write down your plan.

Your baby also relies on you for pretty much everything. It can be overwhelming to think about how much your baby depends on you, but you're creating a beautiful and important bond with them during this time. From your first interactions with your baby, even back when they were in your body, you were building "attachment" with them.[10] Attachment is the relationship between a baby and their caregiver (biological or not) that gives the baby their first feelings of safety, security, and protection.[11] These feelings are the start of relationship patterns that will grow in your baby for the rest of their lives.

This may seem like I'm making things even more overwhelming by reminding you of how important your early contact is for your baby. I don't bring this up to make you feel even more pressure. Rather, I want to relieve some of the pressure you might already be putting on yourself to make this a magical time and to feel an instant connection with your baby. That isn't necessary. It's okay if you don't feel connected or bonded with your baby right away. The attachment you're creating during these early days is more about what you *do* with your baby than how you feel about it. And working on building attachment with your baby actually makes *you* feel better too.

Most importantly, we need to let go of the idea of being a "perfect" mom. There are no perfect moms. The idea of perfection only makes us *all* feel terrible about how we're not measuring up to this impossible standard. We have to let go of our expectation that we have to (or can be) perfect at this and embrace the reality that our goal is to just be *good enough* as moms. Our children don't expect us to be perfect. Since we are the only mom they have or will ever know, they just want *us*. The best we can be for our children is to be ourselves, to let them see us make mistakes and try to do better, and to love them in our imperfect ways.

It's easy to understand why we've internalized this idea of perfection in motherhood. There are countless images on social media of women who look put together, happy, and stress-free in their roles as mothers. It's easy to think that these images are of perfect moms, and that maybe it's the norm to be able to handle everything while looking made-up and in style. This comparison wasn't visually and immediately available to previous generations of moms, so the daily judgment of ourselves as imperfect or substandard moms is a new phenomenon.

None of it is true, though. There are no perfect moms, and those pictures you see on social media are carefully crafted, filtered, and staged to make those moms look effortless and "perfect." The reality is that those moms (if they are actually real people) have had babies who wouldn't stop crying, struggled with feeding or sleeping, and had moments when they didn't know what they're doing. No moms out there feel like they have it all figured out. We have to stop comparing ourselves to an unrealistic ideal so that we can appreciate our efforts in getting through each day.

PRACTICE: *Letting Go of the Idea of the "Perfect" Mom*

First, recognize whether you've thought about how you need to be a "perfect" mom or how other moms seem to be perfect to you. What do you think a "perfect" mom does or doesn't do?

Next, recognize that no one can be perfect and that no mother or parent can do those things you see as "perfect" 100 percent of the time. We all struggle with some aspects of parenting, and every single one of us struggles sometimes.

When you find yourself thinking about an ideal of how you or others "should be" as parents, replace it with the idea of "I'm doing my best" or "We're doing our best." Make this your goal as a parent: to do your best, to improve at things you struggle with, and to love your child in your own imperfect way.

embracing your community

Every time we coo at, smile at, or get close to our baby in other ways, we're helping them to develop their own regulatory system and sync up their internal feelings with the world around them.[12] This is a small but powerful way to build our baby's resilience and ability to feel safe, secure, and loved. Before they can ever learn their ABCs, they're learning about how to soothe themselves, what it feels like and what to do when they feel good and when they don't. This is one of the most important gifts you can give your new baby: to be close and interact with them, even for a little bit each day, so they can internalize how to feel better.

When your baby cries, initially it's because they need something from you. They need to be changed, fed, burped, held, or rocked to sleep. They're basically saying, "I have a need! Is there anyone there to take care of it?" If someone addresses their needs within a reasonable amount of time, your baby feels better—not just because their dirty diaper was changed or because they were fed, but because they build more trust each time that someone is there to take care of them. The more this happens, the more safe and secure your baby will feel. And the more they feel this way, the easier it will be for them to create that feeling within themselves when they need it as they become more independent from you.

There will be times when you can't get to your baby right away, or when someone else is taking care of them, or when your baby may have to cry for a bit. First of all, the longer your baby is alive, the more okay it is if their need isn't met immediately. If you've already built a secure routine for them, then they know someone will come eventually. Second, as long as *someone* comes, that's fine. It doesn't have to be you all the time. This is how babies generalize that other caregivers can be trusted, which is a necessary development if you ever want to leave the house again. It's okay if your partner responds just as often as you do, or even most of the time. What matters most is that your baby learns that someone will take care of them when they need it.

As your baby develops this internal sense and this healthy, secure attachment to you, they'll often show affection to you, and seek comfort from you.[13] These hallmarks of secure attachment confirm that it's crucial to act toward your baby in ways that are affectionate and comforting as much as possible.

The goal is for your baby to see you as a "safe haven," or someone they can reach for when they feel upset, hungry, angry, lonely, tired, etc. You also want your baby to see you as their "secure base," or someone who will watch over them while they go out and explore the world.[14] Both of these are important; as your child grows up, they can form close connections with other people yet feel empowered to be adventurous and discover new things. Incredibly, it's through little interactions with you in these early days that they develop these ideas about the world.

PRACTICE: *Being Your Baby's Safe Haven and Secure Base*

Safe Haven: Create close-up moments that encourage your baby's feelings of safety with you.

- Spend five minutes playing with your baby, and focus on what you're doing with them.
- Allow yourself to do this and nothing else during those five minutes.
- Make eye contact with your baby. Talk to them in a caring, soothing tone.
- Laugh and smile at your baby while you play with them.

In this way, you're building your baby's awareness that you are a safe haven for them.

Secure Base: Practice interactions with your baby while they're a short distance away from you.

- If your baby is in their swing or high chair while you're doing chores or making dinner, play peekaboo or another interactive game.
- Encourage and cheer on your baby as they play or explore on their own.
- Make eye contact with your baby from across the room, say their name, and/or smile and wave with excitement when they look at you.

These interactions build trust in your baby that you're there for them, even when you're not far away.

Giving your baby what they need and helping them form this secure attachment can also be healing and helpful for you. Cuddling with, cooing at, and making eye contact with your baby spurs the release of the hormone oxytocin—the "connection chemical"—in both your baby and you! This is the brain chemical that floods you with feelings of happiness and contentment when you're connected with other people.[15] Affectionate touching, eye contact, and loving words and tone of voice all help our brains produce more oxytocin and feel happier when we're in connection. If you don't feel particularly connected with your baby naturally, acting "as if"—just *doing* the connecting, oxytocin-releasing activities—works to build up the feelings of connection you might be lacking.

Doing the motions of mothering, even when we don't necessarily feel joyful about them, also can be a practice in building your self-esteem. In other words, you can build up your confidence by taking care of your baby. Stepping back from the mundaneness of some of the tasks of parenting and recognizing them as acts of love toward our baby, our partner, and maybe ourselves can make them more rewarding and also much more important.

PRACTICE: *Recognizing That You Deserve Love*

It can be overwhelming to think about how much your baby depends on you. So when you find yourself caught in this thought, shift your focus to how much your baby loves you and how much you deserve that love.

Take a few moments to consider all of the things you've done to take care of your baby today. Maybe you've fed your baby, changed their diaper, rocked them to sleep, sung them a song, and/or taken them for a walk. All of these are acts of love that make you a wonderful parent, especially in the eyes of your baby. Recognize yourself as your baby sees you: as the most amazing parent they've ever had!

CREATING ATTACHMENT WHEN YOU DON'T FEEL SECURE

You may be thinking, *I wonder if I'm not "securely attached," because I definitely struggle with this!* It's indisputably true that we carry our own early experiences with us into parenting. So if our caregivers struggled to provide us with that feeling of safety and security when we were young, it affects us even as adults. This might be because our early caregivers— whether they were mothers, fathers, or someone else—were physically or emotionally absent or inconsistent when we were young, possibly because of their own mental health issues, financial struggles, illness, or other strains. We can also struggle with connection if we've gone through difficult relationships that involved abuse, trauma, or loss.

Research suggests that there are three main types of attachment: secure, anxious, and avoidant. Most people (over 50 percent) fall into the secure attachment category. These folks may have received what they believe to be "good enough" parenting when they were young and now feel reasonably able to navigate relationships as adults and comfortable with being close to others. Another 20 percent of adults fall into the anxious attachment category. This means that they may have had inconsistent or unpredictable caregiving or relationships, where they weren't sure whether someone would be there for them when they needed it. This can translate into anxiety in adult relationships, such as wanting closeness but being unsure of how to get it without feeling or appearing needy. Another 25 percent of adults are avoidant, meaning they have learned not to rely on others from a young age and now feel uncomfortable being close with others. A final 3 to 5 percent might fall into a combined anxious-avoidant or disorganized attachment style, meaning that they have elements of both anxiety and avoidance in relationships.[16]

Paying attention to your feelings about attachment becomes important when you have a baby. You're forming some of those early patterns and expectations with them now, and those patterns are based on your own upbringing and preferences. It's okay if you notice that you fall more into the anxious or avoidant categories in your own attachment style. That doesn't necessarily mean that your baby also will. Focusing on consistently connecting with them builds security even if you don't feel especially secure yourself. Here are some ways to practice this, depending on your tendencies.

PRACTICE: *Building Security and Attachment*

If You Feel Secure in Your Attachment . . .

Think about how good it feels to be close and connected with someone. Close your eyes and sense what it feels like in your body. See this closeness as a strength that you want to share with your baby. Think about how building this wonderful feeling within yourself also allows you to emit that feeling to those around you. Being near you allows your baby to grow that feeling within them as well. Connect with your baby consciously out of this loving feeling at least once a day.

If You Feel Anxious in Your Attachment . . .

It's okay if you notice that you feel anxious in your relationships or with your baby. When you notice that you feel this way, inhale deeply and exhale completely. Maybe even hold the breath out a little longer. This soothes your nervous system and calms you down in a powerful way. Do this a few times to feel calmer, then connect with your baby during this calm state. Get close and talk with them in a quiet tone. Make eye contact. Sing or laugh near them. These cues build a happy, secure connection with your baby. Allow yourself to feel calm and happy during these moments as well.

Your challenge is to build in moments of calm and peacefulness at least once a day and to allow yourself to truly be in the moment with your baby.

If You Feel Avoidant in Your Attachment . . .

It is okay if you feel a little uncomfortable with closeness in relationships or with your baby. When you notice that you are feeling this way, close your eyes and place a hand on your chest, near your heart. Feel the weight of your hand there, and allow the muscles to relax. Take a few deep breaths with your hand on your chest, and allow yourself to feel more at ease. Now connect with your baby during this more relaxed state—get close, talk with them in a quiet tone, make eye contact, maybe sing or laugh near them. These cues are what build a happy, secure connection with your baby. Allow yourself to feel calm and happy during these moments as well!

Your challenge is to allow yourself to feel close and connected to your baby at least once a day. Relax your tension to do this, and allow yourself to notice how you feel softer and more at ease when you have these moments.

It can be helpful to know if you had disruptions in attachment during your early years, but that knowledge won't necessarily solve anything for you now. What *can* help you form more stable attachments with your baby and with others is recognizing where you struggle and making efforts to do things differently. Even doing the above practices regularly and in small doses can help you feel more secure in your attachments over time.

You may feel stressed when your baby needs or wants you and have a hard time bringing yourself to connect with, cuddle with, and feel close to them. Or you may feel anxiety about anticipating your baby's needs, which gets in the way of your connection with them. Though we each struggle with different aspects of bonding and building attachment, the solution to each struggle is similar: focus on being present, right now, in this moment.

embracing your community

PRACTICE: *Mindfully Engaging with Your Baby*

Spend five minutes playing or being with your baby and focus on what you're doing with them. Allow yourself to do this and nothing else for these five minutes. Get close with them, make eye contact, talk with them, and kiss or touch them gently. Focus only on being with your baby for these few moments.

Later, reflect on how you felt while you were doing this activity. What felt good? Did anything feel awkward or strange? What would you like to try differently next time?

It's easy for us to live in our own thoughts and worries instead of experiencing the feelings of connecting with our baby. If we allow ourselves to just be with them, connected with them, it actually feels pretty good! This is the power of being present. Instead of focusing on what we're worried about, living in judgment, or doubting that we're doing a good job, if we can just *be* with our babies, we can feel the power of that connection and loving feeling. The more often you practice this, the easier it will become to let go of the worries or doubts for a while and be more present in the now.

COMMON POST-BABY RELATIONSHIP ISSUES

Earlier, we talked about how your relationship with your partner is changing and may be strained after having your baby. Improving your partner relationship might not be at the top of your priority list with a new baby at home. However, that relationship also needs some attention or effort to endure this trying time for the two of you.

If you and your partner both feel stressed by the new responsibilities of parenting, this kind of stress could amplify any problems that already exist in your relationship. These can include communication, conflict, connection and intimacy, finances, roles, and responsibilities. These common relationship problems don't just go away on their own. If any of these were already issues, you're most likely noticing them more than ever now that another person— your baby—is in the relationship.

Here are the main points of conflict or argument in relationships after having a baby.

ROLES AND RESPONSIBILITIES

Responsibilities change after a baby comes because there is MORE TO DO! Even if you and your partner had established good routines before your baby arrived, the balance will be upset. You'll have to reconfigure things. You have to handle many more daily tasks now: diapers, feeding, laundry, washing dishes, sleep schedules, bathing, and managing child care, just to name a few. And while you might fall into a natural rhythm with these tasks, you also might not. So you may need to have a discussion with your partner about how to divide responsibilities and child care in a way that makes the most sense for you and your family situation.

This can come up in unexpected ways. For example, Bria was pregnant with her first child with her partner, who had two other children from a previous relationship. During her pregnancy, Bria found her partner's experience with parenting comforting. They knew what they were doing, and this made her feel more calm about the birth and parenting experience. After she gave birth, though, Bria found herself wanting to parent in a different way than her partner did; and she started to find their experience a hindrance (and a little annoying). She wanted to talk about doing things differently, but she felt she had helped establish a hierarchy while she was pregnant that now put her partner at an unfair advantage. Ultimately, Bria found it freeing and empowering to claim her role and share her feelings with her partner about doing things differently. She communicated about it in a way that strengthened their relationship overall.

INTIMACY AND SEX

Your sense of connection with your partner is going to be different after having a baby. This is because, first of all, you're physically going through a major recovery period. Second, a new and needy person has entered your and your partner's relationship! It's totally normal to lose your interest in sex after having a baby.[17] Not only has your body been through a major trauma—regardless of how or where you gave birth—but also, your entire life and priorities have shifted. It takes a while to put physical intimacy back on the list. It's okay to talk with your partner about slowly returning to normal with your sex drive and to let them know that the physical and emotional recovery period varies for every new mom. Letting your partner know that this isn't personal—that it's not about them or anything they are or aren't doing—can help them be more understanding and patient with the process as well.

PARENTING STYLES

While you and your partner may have had some ideas about how each of you would parent based on personalities and families, you're now seeing it in reality—and some contrasts are likely. Differences in parenting styles will likely come up again and again as your child grows up and goes through their unique phases, needing distinct things from you as parents. That's why it's a good idea, either early in your baby's life or even while you're pregnant, to discuss with your partner how you'll talk through differences in parenting styles. Each of you are likely to be most comfortable with whatever style you grew up with or saw in your own parent(s). Talk about what each of you learned from your parents about parenting as well as any things you want to preserve or resist. Having this discussion will be easier if you're starting from an understanding that differences will come up between you and your partner, and that neither of you is right or wrong. Rather, both of you may be responding from different instincts and different things each of you have learned.

MONEY

We all know that children come with some financial strain. A lot of times, this is an area that was already contentious between partners to begin with. Just as with parenting styles, you and your partner likely learned different ways of handling money, and you may have been drawn to each other because of these differences. Studies have shown that opposites often attract even in how partners handle finances. People who are more reckless with their spending are often drawn to those who are tighter with their money, and vice versa.[18] Where conflict often arises is when you feel like your way is right, and your partner's is wrong. (Or, in other cases, you may think your partner's way is better.) Practice the skills of nonjudgment you learned earlier in this book; and recognize that there is no right or wrong way of handling money, but that there are *different* ways. Talking through financial matters from this lens can help you lower your emotional reactivity when you feel either right or wrong and allow yourself to just discuss things *as they are*— different.

We'll talk more about how to handle difficult conversations about these and other sources of conflict with your partner in the next chapter. The point is that you have to communicate about those issues with your partner if you're going to be able to support each other in the ways you'll need to through the first years of parenthood.

TAPPING INTO YOUR PARTNER'S SUPPORT

Your partner might also be helpful to you in different ways during this time. They might offer support by helping with certain tasks. There are so many household and baby-care tasks to do that it can easily feel overwhelming unless you have help. Your partner might also offer emotional support and make you feel good about yourself as a mother. Finally, they might help with problem-solving or figuring things out, which can also feel overwhelming for moms to do on their own after having a baby. Sometimes a supportive person can help you talk through the different options for feeding or sleep training or research different medications for when your baby is sick.[19] Any of these methods may feel supportive to you. You may also find that you need one type of support most often from your partner. If you realize you need something specific, let your partner know! No one is a mind reader, and your partner might need (and appreciate) a little direction in how to be most helpful to you right now.

Allowing yourself to open up to support can be hard if your comfort zone lies in doing everything yourself. Opening up like this can make you feel vulnerable, which can be scary. Brené Brown reframes vulnerability as courage; it takes a pretty brave person to open up and talk about what you think and feel. We'll talk more about this in the next chapter, but here is a practice to help you think about vulnerability as strength.

PRACTICE: *Being Strong and Vulnerable*

Spend some time thinking about vulnerability and how the act of opening up and letting others know what you're thinking and feeling is a strength instead of a weakness. Feel what you normally feel when you think about being vulnerable. For example, you may feel your heart racing or experience tightness in your chest. Notice what it feels like for you. Next, imagine yourself taking off this armor, and focus on the feeling of strength within yourself. This is the strength that you need— not armor, but openness. Let it fill your heart and your center. Consider how you can act out of this strength instead of hiding behind false armor.

The most important thing about social support is that you realize you're not alone in this. Early motherhood is hard. It may even be the hardest time in your life. That means it's an incredibly hard time in the lives of all mothers— and we can bear the burden of it better together than alone. So rally your partner and teammates, your friends and family, and your supporters near and far. Let them know how you're doing. Recognize that it's important to tell people how you're doing, because how you're doing *matters*. In the next chapter, we'll talk about all of the hard things that you'll face, and it will all be easier if you have a team of supporters with you.

CHAPTER 3 CHECKLIST

Here are the practices
you learned in this chapter:

1. Reaching Out
2. Reflecting on Your Supports
3. Building Up Your Support System
4. Seeing Yourself from Your Baby's Perspective
5. Letting Go of the Idea of the "Perfect" Mom
6. Being Your Baby's Safe Haven and Secure Base
7. Recognizing that You Deserve Love
8. Building Security and Attachment
9. Mindfully Engaging with Your Baby
10. Being Strong and Vulnerable

Pick two favorites from the list above. Write them on a piece of paper and tape it to your bathroom mirror. Make the practices that were useful to you a part of your daily routine, and consider marking the ones that were harder to connect with so you can explore them further or try them again later. Practice doesn't make perfect, but it helps to make it a habit and deepen the positive effects the more you try these exercises.

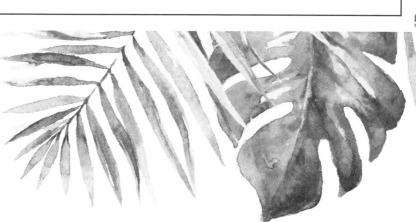

4

Building Your Confidence:

From
"I Can't Do This"
to
"I Can Do Hard Things"

WE'RE REQUIRED TO DO a lot of hard things in early motherhood. Most of these things have to do with keeping a tiny human alive, even when you feel as though you haven't mastered how to keep yourself alive. The goal of this chapter is to talk you through some of these difficult undertakings so that you feel like you're not just surviving through them, but that you can actually enjoy yourself and this time in your life a little more.

Two mindsets will be important as you prepare yourself to do hard things: one of acceptance and one of willingness. Practicing acceptance is about approaching yourself and the external world with a caring openness. This means looking at yourself—including the things you like and don't like about yourself—and recognizing that whatever you find is okay. It just is. You can't change yourself by hating things about you, and you can't change things at all if you can't recognize them for what they are. Willingness then opens our minds and hearts to allow for change, instead of resisting or closing to it.

We opened this book with a practice about openness and acceptance. Now let's focus this positive, accepting energy toward yourself and your faults, flaws, and weaknesses. We all have them. Being mean to ourselves about them doesn't make them go away. It only makes us feel miserable about ourselves. So let's practice self-acceptance and the willingness to face and do hard things.

PRACTICE: *Inhaling Self-Acceptance and Exhaling Willingness*

Close your eyes, and call to mind a feeling of love and acceptance. Take a few deep breaths, and let each one fill and open your heart. Focus on the feeling of acceptance for a few breaths, and then extend that feeling toward yourself, strengths and weaknesses and all. Whatever you are thinking or feeling about yourself, extend a feeling of love and acceptance toward it. Breathe in acceptance and love, and breathe out openness and willingness to work on things—and know that you're worth it.

Facing your challenges—both in taking care of your baby and in working on the things you want to feel better about—will require you to bring back that nonjudgmental stance we talked about in chapter 2. There are a lot of reasons for why we judge ourselves more harshly than we judge other people. We may feel shame about things we've done or gone through. We may be comparing ourselves to the "perfect" personas we see online. Or we may be particularly hard on ourselves because the voice in our heads tells us that we can do better.

Why should we talk about facing our problems? Research suggests that having realistic expectations about motherhood helps your mental health.[1] If you think things are going to be all rosy and great and then they're not, it's a harder shift to make than if you expect things to be hard and frustrating and then they are (or aren't!). Also, when you're home alone with your baby, you can feel isolated and think no one else has ever had it so bad or felt so bad about things. Trust me—*all* new moms have had it that bad and felt that bad, and we all have wondered whether it was like this for others.

Something that has been incredibly helpful and freeing for me in parenting is *letting go of expectations*. This is about setting yourself free from worries about how things will turn out, or that there is a certain measure of success. Letting go of the outcome—or the idea that it "has to be" a certain way—frees you up to do the hard things. That way, you aren't digging in your heels because it "shouldn't be so hard" or because you think you have to follow the same formula as so-and-so, since her kids turned out to be geniuses (or whatever). Letting go of expectations might even allow you to enjoy the journey, including the moments that are hard. They're also just moments, and each is the only one of its kind that we'll get. Here is a way to switch yourself into this kind of thinking whenever you're pulled by expectations or dreading something that might be hard.

PRACTICE: *Letting Go of Expectations*

If you're dreading something or regretting that you've fallen short of a certain expectation (either your own or someone else's), focus on what expectation you're holding. Are you thinking that you have to do something a certain way? Are you holding on to an ideal of what is "best"?

When you have identified the expectation, take a deep breath in and exhale it. Visualize the expectation flying away from you. It's not tethered to you, and it doesn't need to weigh on you or fill you with dread or regret. Instead, it blows away easily, drifting into the air, far away until you can't see it anymore.

Finally, think about the thing you're dreading or regretting, and see if it feels a little different. If not, you may need to exhale away other expectations that might be tied to it. Repeat this until all of the expectations are gone. What needs attention now feels light and easy. Now you can face it without that weight. Maybe you can even enjoy or be more fully open to it.

We'll talk about a number of things that you'll likely face in these early months of parenthood in a little bit. First, let's discuss something that usually gets in our way as we deal with these big, heavy priorities: self-doubt, the fear that we aren't good enough, smart enough, or whatever enough to make this decision for ourselves or our baby.

It's important to recognize when self-doubt slips in. It signals to you that something is taking you away from your core self, which knows and has confidence in the fact that you're the very best person to make decisions for your own life. Self-doubt, like any feeling, isn't good or bad. Rather, it lets you know you need to pay attention to something. When self-doubt creeps in, it's a sign to concentrate on your strengths—because you have many!—and to spend time building up your confidence about the things you absolutely can do and are the best person to do for your baby and your family.

PRACTICE: *Focusing on Your Strengths*

When you notice feelings of self-doubt or thoughts such as *I'm no good at this* or *Other moms seem so much better than I am,* write down three of your strengths. If you can't think of any, consider the praise you've received. Find your strengths there.

Think about how each of these strengths benefits you as a parent. Write down your thoughts about each one.

Finally, write down an affirmation to remind yourself of your strengths when things get tough and you struggle to remember them. It can start with the phrase "I am . . ." and then draw on the list of strengths you came up with. If it's hard to find an affirmation that fits, you can write, "I am doing my best."

Keep this list of strengths and affirmations somewhere accessible, and look back at it when you doubt yourself and your abilities.

You'll notice a theme as we talk about the hard things you'll face: that ultimately, you are the one to make these decisions. There is no single theory or philosophy about parenting that applies to every parent, family, or situation. So the best you can do is to trust yourself to sift through all of the information that's out there, see how each bit applies to your life and situation, and then make the best decision for you. It doesn't mean that you won't make missteps or try something that won't work well. It just means that you're the expert on you. We'll talk more about developing this self-trust in the next chapter. If this is something you struggle with, don't skip that part of the book.

For now, let's look at the messages and challenges you'll likely face as you make these hard choices. Feel free to hop to whichever section(s) are of interest to you, and know that there is a practice in each one to help you feel grounded in your own ability to handle whatever life (or your baby) throws at you.

TAKING CARE OF YOUR BABY

Figuring out how to take care of your baby can be the hardest part of new motherhood. While some new moms naturally feel their maternal instincts and know what their baby needs, many others feel like they have no idea what they're doing for the first several months. One new mom I know told me how she felt surprised that she didn't just *know* what her baby needed when she brought her home from the hospital. She hadn't been prepared to *not* know what to do when her baby cried. Over time, it got easier for her to recognize her baby's different cries and to establish a routine of things to try, from checking the baby's diaper to knowing whether she's hungry or tired. But as she and other new moms often discover, sometimes everything can be just right and taken care of, yet your baby will cry anyway!

It's important to give yourself credit and grace (which means reserving judgment) for just keeping at it and *trying* through this phase. It's okay if you don't have a natural maternal instinct. I would argue that most of us don't, we're just developing it along with our new babies, and some moms and babies catch on more quickly than others. The point is that you do have a maternal instinct because you are your baby's mom, and you know your baby better than anyone.

PRACTICE: *Finding Your Maternal Instinct*

If you don't feel like you have a strong maternal instinct, think about what you believe a maternal instinct is. Consider whether you might be defining it in unrealistic or unhelpful ways, like "always knowing what my baby needs" or "not getting upset when my baby cries or needs something." Think about more helpful ways of thinking about maternal instincts, such as "continually learning about my baby and how to take care of them."

With this definition in mind, think about what you've learned about your baby in the last few days. Were there any times when you tried something new and it worked well? Or when something that used to work didn't work anymore? (The latter will happen as your baby moves in and out of new phases.) Each time this happens, you learn something new about your baby. These small lessons help you develop your maternal instinct.

Then consciously focus on the things you're learning about your baby and how to take care of them, instead of what you feel like you *don't* know. Cultivate a feeling of happiness and satisfaction each time you learn something new as a mom, and see this as progress and even joy that you're feeling in being a mother.

You've likely already faced lots of opinions, advice, and conflicting data about how to feed your baby and how to help them learn how to sleep through the night. All of this conflicting information only makes us feel anxious because there are so many choices and vehement opinions that we're sure to encounter what seems like valid evidence and yet heated disagreement on all sides.

As far as how to feed your baby, let's break down the current medical information as simply as possible: *A fed baby is best.* This means that, if you're feeding your baby, no matter what you decide is right for them, you're doing a great job. This is now supported by the American Academy of Pediatrics,[2] which is the ultimate resource for information on all types of feeding for your child when they're a baby and then as they grow.

The benefits of breastfeeding have been well documented.[3] However, many moms out there are unable to breastfeed (exclusively or otherwise) for a variety of reasons: low milk supply, medications they need to take, an infectious disease or addiction on their part, birth issues with the baby that prevent latching or feeding, the need for a feeding tube or supplements, or personal preference. If you choose or need to do something different to feed your baby, you don't need to feel guilty. You're putting your, your baby's, and your family's unique needs first—and as I said earlier, a fed baby is best of all!

Helping your baby learn to sleep is also a controversial topic. Few babies sleep through the night, at least during the first few months.[4] This becomes problematic because, of course, if they aren't sleeping for long intervals, their parents aren't sleeping either. New parents must go to great lengths to get a basic amount of sleep. And you, too, need sleep! You won't sleep as long or as well as you did before you had a baby, so keep realistic expectations. Some parents handle frequent waking more readily, and other parents can't tolerate interruptions in their sleep. This leads to a wide range of opinions and methods for encouraging babies to sleep, from "cry it out" methods to "no-cry" methods and everything in between. Supporters of each method are often fervent about their preferences. But no one technique works for everyone, and no one method is the only right answer. Ultimately, you'll need to figure out what works best for you and your family and then avoid shaming others for choosing differently than you.

Again deferring to the experts, the American Academy of Pediatrics doesn't endorse any specific method for helping babies sleep. They do, however, suggest basic ways to encourage sleep. These include the following:

- Avoid overstimulating your baby when they wake during the night to ensure an easier transition back to sleep
- Interact with your baby most often during the day to encourage their day-night/sleep-wake signals to align
- Put your baby to bed when they're drowsy but still awake
- Wait a few minutes to respond when your baby cries or fusses to encourage them to fall back asleep on their own[5]

These suggestions are moderate and suited for most families. So you may come to the conclusion that any methods that are more extreme than these probably aren't for you. In tougher situations, you may want to seek out a medical professional to advise you.

The hard part about making these (and other) parenting choices for your family is that you'll encounter people who are convinced to their very core and have science to prove that their method is the only one that works and that all others damage babies. Their strong opinions may also be fueled by their desire for you to choose the method they chose, because they'll feel validated for their choice if others go along with them. This is the trap: we have to *self-validate* without relying too heavily on others to make the choice for us or putting anyone down for making a different choice. We all want to feel that we've made the right choice. But just as there is no perfect mom, there is no one right choice. Many different choices might turn out the same way in the end; and no one way is right for every family, baby, or situation.

It can be hard to know what your instincts are when you're surrounded by strong opinions and people who might feel or seem very "right." It can also be hard to balance your emotional reactions to your baby's sleeplessness or any feelings that come up when someone is vehement about their beliefs. These people often use rational arguments and convincing or condescending tones. The truth is that both emotions and rational thinking are important and valid to any decision you make. Dialectical behavior therapy calls this balance between emotions and rational thinking your "wise mind." Making decisions from your wise mind—and we all have one!—means tuning in to our feelings and recognizing them as valid while also bringing in reason, science, and rational arguments.

PRACTICE: *Listening to Your Maternal Instinct*

1. If you're struggling to make a decision based on your instinct or intuition, take a few minutes to sit quietly and notice what you are feeling.
2. Put a label to the feeling(s): "I am feeling _____."
3. Write down the feelings you're able to name: _____
   _____
4. Tap into your rational mind, and think about why you're feeling this way. Maybe you can label it like this: "I am feeling _____ because _____."
5. Allow the feelings and thoughts to come to you freely. Don't try to stop or correct them.
6. List the rational pieces of the decision in front of you. What are the factors that you think are important? What facts might play into the decision?
7. Think through the possible decisions or outcomes that are in front of you. List the various possible decisions, and see how they fit with the feelings and thoughts you identified.

If balancing your emotions with rational thinking or tapping into your "wise mind" is one of your big challenges, you may want to look into *The Dialectical Behavior Therapy Skills Workbook* by Matthew McKay, Jeffrey C. Wood, and Jeffrey Brantley.

COMMUNICATING WITH YOUR PARTNER

As we talked about in the previous chapter, you and your partner will likely experience a lot of new or amplified conflicts as you both adjust to parenthood. Roles, responsibilities, intimacy, finances, and parenting all put a huge strain on your relationship. These conflicts show you where those tension points might have been in the past, but in new ways.

The first step in tackling any of these relationship issues is to take a look at which part of the issue at hand is yours to change. No relationship problem is completely yours to fix, but you're never completely free from the repair either. In every interaction, a part of it is yours and another part is the other person's; and while it might be easier to identify what the other person needs to change, that isn't the part that you have control over. The only thing you can do to solve a relationship issue is to work on your part and communicate with your partner about theirs.

If communication is a tricky issue for you and your partner, start by looking at where you have trouble communicating. Maybe you don't like bringing up hard topics. Or maybe you feel too vulnerable when you begin a conversation about something delicate like finances or emotions. The most helpful thing to start with is what you're willing and committed to change for and within yourself.

PRACTICE: *Recognizing Your Part in a Relationship Conflict*

1. Think about situations where you have trouble communicating with your partner.
2. Identify a few different scenarios, and consider the common denominator for you in those situations.
3. Try to boil down the issue you have into a simple, nonjudgmental statement. An example might be, "I prefer not to be the one to introduce a sensitive topic."
4. Look for judgment words in your statement, like *bad, shouldn't, better, terrible*. Then choose more neutral terms to replace any judgment words. Instead of thinking that you're bad at something, is it possible that you'd like to do it in a different way?
5. Identify what you'd like to do differently. Again, look for judgment words and replace them with neutral ones, or challenge yourself to think about the difference you'd like to see.
6. Review what you'd like to do differently, and see if it's something you can commit to trying.
7. Imagine what it will feel like to do that thing differently the next time you talk with your partner.
8. Remind yourself to feel a sense of accomplishment or self-celebration when you finally do it!

Communicating with your partner about their role in the issue can be challenging. It's a delicate balance to bring up something that someone else needs to work on without coming across as nagging or blaming. Here is where assertive communication can be so helpful. Some people have a negative reaction to the word *assertive*. However, assertiveness is a balanced communication style that doesn't give all of the power to the other person or take all of the power and control from them. Assertive communication is about asserting your own feelings *while* allowing for the other person's. This has also been called nonviolent communication, because it is a way of being open and authentic to your own self and empathetic toward others.

It's easy to assume that we know what our partner is thinking or how they're going to respond. Maybe we put a lot of effort into trying to craft the "perfect" argument. Or maybe we anticipate what our partner will say and make it so that they can't argue or question our point of view. The trap here is that we don't need to argue our own feelings. Our feelings are valid for the mere fact that we have them. We aren't crafting an argument; instead, we're planning to be open about how we feel. That way, our partner knows our feelings and we can try a different pattern or to find a solution together. Thinking this way about communicating with your partner makes it less like a scary proposition we have to prepare for and more like an exciting undertaking we have to help ourselves feel ready for. Here is a practice to help us prepare.

PRACTICE: *Communicating Using Assertive Language*

Think about an issue you'd like to discuss with your partner. See if you can frame the issue using these sentences. Writing out the sentences ahead of time can be helpful!

Identify a specific feeling that you have in this situation: "I feel _____."

Be specific about where your feeling comes from as well as what happens or what is said that leads you to have this feeling:
"When _____."

Be open about where your feeling comes from, if you interpret something in a certain way, or if you have some personal history that's important for your partner to know: "Because _____."

Offer a possible solution that would feel better to you in those situations, or an invitation for you and your partner to figure out a solution together: "I would like _____."

Plan a time to talk to your partner, and use these statements as your starting point. Try not to assume that you know what your partner's reaction will be. Let go of trying to control what happens after you say these things. After you say them, be open to listening to your partner's response, and see if there is a way you can come to an agreement about what you'll change going forward.

WORKING WITH YOUR PARTNER AS A TEAM

There are so many tasks that come with a new baby that you might find that you and your partner fall into a habit of working within your own bubbles. Often our tendency is to play "zone defense," with each partner staying in their own lane and managing as best they can with just the things each can handle on their own. But if we do this all the time, without reconnecting or communicating with our partner, we're not actually playing on the same team. This kind of approach is very separating and isolating; and over time, it will likely lead to feelings of loneliness and resentment because you don't feel supported in what you're doing or see what your partner is doing.

Having "zones" might be necessary to get everything done. So, the key is to find ways to stay connected or to check in with your partner to make sure you're still working as a team, even while physically separated or focused on your own part of the tasks. Basketball players can't *only* focus on their own zone, or they would have no idea what is going on with their teammates or with the game in general. They have to see their teammates; know where the ball is; connect with each other to receive, assist, or pass; and ultimately stay focused on the goal, which is getting the ball to the net together.

Because this balance of zones and teamwork may be new to you and your partner, it may take conscious effort and work to stay connected (or to reconnect, if you've fallen into these habits already). This means having a discussion about what you want your teamwork and communication to look like. Plan how you'll check in with your partner and how you'll know it's the best time for support or relief.

PRACTICE: *Keeping the Team Together*

Find ways to connect with your partner when you feel isolated or lonely in your baby-related responsibilities. It might be as simple as eye contact, a supportive smile, or a pat on the shoulder when you're both in the middle of different things. This can be useful when the baby is having a meltdown that requires you to work together, or when you might be focused on your own "zones" to finish tasks around the house.

After the hard situation passes, take the following steps:

1. Take a few minutes to connect with your partner. What just happened? Consider this your debrief or "review of the tapes."

2. Talk about what went well, what didn't go so well, and what you'd like to do the next time something like this happens.

3. Communicate your feelings, and leave space for your partner to share theirs.

4. Talk about how the two of you can support each other when things feel like this.

5. End with affirmations for each other (e.g., a statement such as, "Good job with _____," a hug, or pat on the back).

Remind yourself early and often that you're in this together and that your goal is the same: to get through these hard moments and feel better about them each time.

building your confidence

DEALING WITH YOUR BABY'S ILLNESS OR MEDICAL ISSUES

Your baby's health is likely one of the most important things to you. It's understandable; one of a mother's most prevalent worries is about her baby's health. Even the healthiest babies are likely to get sick up to twelve times during their first year of life, with illnesses such as colds, ear infections, and gastrointestinal issues.[6] Each time will probably worry you because all of the firsts are new and unknown, and you might feel you're expected to read your baby's signals more than is reasonably possible at this stage. Luckily, pediatricians are more than used to parents' worries and are willing to respond to calls and let you know what to do or watch for. You should absolutely have a pediatrician that you feel comfortable with and whose advice you trust. If you don't have one, call around. It's most important that you have an ongoing physician who will answer your questions while your baby is young and who understands the importance of this time in your and your baby's life and can make you feel as comfortable and secure as possible when you have questions or concerns.

Beyond normal illnesses, research shows that 70 percent of preterm babies and 10 to 15 percent of *all* babies will spend time in hospitals' NICU.[7] Unless you knew you were going to give birth early or knew other moms whose babies spent time in the NICU, you might not have thought much about this stressful, anxiety-inducing situation while you were reading other "what to expect" books and thinking about your birth experience. Seeing and spending time with your baby while they're in the NICU is hard. This might not be the early experience you had envisioned for the two of you; and you'll probably have a lot of fears about what will happen, what procedures are needed, how long your baby will need to be in the NICU, what you can and can't do to help, and what the outcome will be. Many things are out of your control in this situation. Practicing acceptance may be the only thing you can do to ease your fears and concerns about your baby's health.

PRACTICE: *Accepting the Things You Can't Control*

Start by calming your nervous system using deep breathing: in for four counts, out for six counts, holding for a pause after your exhale. Do this five to ten times until you feel that your state of mind is calmer. This can help you pull yourself out of fight-or-flight mode and into the present moment, to a place where you can lower your defenses and open up more easily.

Think about your current situation and any parts of it that are out of your control. This may include what other people say, think, or do, or the timeline or outcome of the situation. If you notice that you're clenching up or that you want to hold on to or figure out the aspects that are out of your control, exhale and relax that part of you.

Allow yourself to feel open and to accept the parts of the situation that are out of your control. Maybe you can even feel warm and inviting toward them. If you can't, just allow them to be, without using your precious energy to resist them or fix them. Just allow them to be.

Practice noticing those aspects that are out of your control from a calm, open, accepting place. Notice what this feels like in your body.

Accepting the parts of the situation you can't control might be enough. If that feels helpful to you, try it each time you find yourself clenching or trying to control things you actually can't.

If you feel like you're craving resolution or action, turn your attention to the parts of the situation you *can* control. This may include your own actions, thoughts, and attitude; distractions; and ways in which you reach out to others for support. Then put all of your energy toward doing self-care, changing your thinking, and reaching out in the ways that you want to and will feel good about.

When you find yourself worrying or angry about the things you *can't* control, remind yourself to turn your attention and energy back to this list—the things you *can* control and that make you feel powerful instead of powerless.

GOING BACK TO WORK

About 72 percent of new moms will go back to work after having a baby, and they often experience mixed emotions.[8] You may be excited to get out of the house, think about something else, and interact with your coworkers (other grown-ups!). You may also feel really sad or anxious about leaving your baby in someone else's care. It can be stressful to be away from your baby for your workday. Many of us feel a combination of eager and uneasy as we return to work.

This is again a struggle of a new role. Sometimes you try to fit yourself back into a role that doesn't necessarily accommodate your new baby, life, and priorities. Even if you return to the same job after having a baby, you may have left as a person who could stay a few minutes late if needed and are now returning as someone who can't because of child care. Maybe you left as a person who could attend three-hour meetings and are returning as a mom who needs to pump at least once every few hours, in a private room, when your office is shared or open. Most importantly, maybe you left as a person whose whole focus could be on work for eight hours a day and are returning a person who now has a child you often think about, want to be with, and need to plan for throughout your day.

Having to split our time between working and mothering often makes us feel like we're not doing a good job in either role. Over half of working mothers (53 percent) say that being a working parent makes it harder to be a "good" parent. Also, 50 percent of working mothers say that being a parent makes it harder to advance at work.[9] We're judging what makes a "good" parent or worker based on a scale that probably holds someone who has fewer other roles as the ideal. In this case, we're already knocked down a peg on this perfectionistic measure of a mom or worker just by being both. If we see a stay-at-home mom as the "best" mom and a full-time worker who isn't a parent as the "best" worker, we obviously won't measure up. Our time, attention, and priorities are automatically split more than this fictional "best" person.

This is a problem of judgment, either by us or by our workplace. If we get rid of this ridiculous idea that there is a "best" kind of worker or parent and recognize that real people *always* have divisions in their time, attention, and priorities, this conflict might fizzle away. We may actually see the benefits of holding multiple priorities or understanding this multitude of roles.

Another reason why we find it hard to be "good" at both roles is because it feels hard to accept less than 100-percent focus on either our baby or our job, either from ourselves or from messages we get from our workplace. Maybe you prided yourself on your ability to focus and get things done at work, and now it feels like your work ethic has plummeted because you spend some of your work time thinking about your baby or other things. Or maybe you work in a place where those who don't have competing interests are rewarded with raises or promotions, so it feels like you'll never get ahead while your baby is on your mind. These are natural conflicts, and ones that won't necessarily go away on their own because they live inside your mind. The best way to work through them is to allow for flexibility and change in your priorities so that you can adapt with them instead of holding yourself to previous standards or someone else's unattainable measurement.

PRACTICE: *Allowing for Flexibility as You Go Back to Work*

As you prepare to go back to work, or after your first experience back at work, reflect on the difficult balance you're carrying. Allow yourself to appreciate the weight of it as well as appreciate yourself for carrying it. Then think about whether there are any expectations you could allow yourself to relax. Recognize whether you're measuring yourself by someone else's standards (and whether that someone else has a baby at home) or by the standard of your pre-baby self. Neither is reasonable, so put them down.

Practice giving yourself permission to shift your focus, attention, and priorities during your work time and at home. You have multiple roles, so you get to have multiple priorities. It's okay if they shift back and forth throughout the day. Sometimes you'll be more focused on your baby. Other times you'll be more focused on your work, your partner, or other things. Allow for these shifts to happen without judgment. If you feel you need to bring your attention back to work, home, your baby, or your partner, bring it back gently and with kindness toward yourself. Of course your attention will wander. You're balancing roles. Recognize that you're doing your best and establishing a new flow that will serve the new you at work and at home in ways that are fluid and continuing to develop.

DEALING WITH POSTPARTUM DEPRESSION OR ANXIETY

As we discussed earlier in this book, postpartum depression (also known as PPD) affects somewhere between 10 and 20 percent of mothers, and one in ten partners.[10,11] Postpartum anxiety is also an issue for many, affecting about one in ten mothers.[12] These are longer-lasting periods of depression or worry/anxiety than the baby blues, which we discussed in chapter 1. Rather, these are diagnosable mental health conditions that may need to be treated by a mental health professional or therapist.

POSTPARTUM DEPRESSION

Here are the symptoms to look for if you think you're struggling with postpartum depression:

- Feelings of sadness, hopelessness, or emptiness
- Anger or irritability
- The urge to cry more than usual or for no apparent reason
- Difficulty with concentration, memory, or making decisions
- Difficulty with sleeping or appetite
- Loss of interest in activities you used to enjoy
- Restlessness or fatigue
- Lack of interest or emotional attachment with baby
- Negative thoughts about your own ability to take care of your baby
- Thoughts about harming yourself or your baby[13]

NOTE: If you have any thoughts about harming yourself or your baby, please reach out for help. You can call the Postpartum Support International (PSI) helpline at 1-800-944-4773 or text them at that same number (for English-speaking users) or 971-420-0294 (for Spanish-speaking users). You can also visit the PSI website at www.postpartum.net to look up local resources in the US and internationally.

Feeling moody, up-and-down, and even crying for no reason are all normal after giving birth. You don't necessarily need to worry if you're experiencing some of the symptoms on this list. It doesn't mean you have postpartum depression or another mental health issue. But if several of these symptoms last for two weeks or more, you may benefit from seeking treatment for postpartum depression. Again, you're not alone. Up to one in every five new mothers will experience postpartum depression. It's absolutely something that can be treated and can get better.

Therapy for postpartum depression isn't weird or scary. It often helps you identify your negative thoughts and find ways to be kinder to yourself. One new mom I know talked about going to therapy after she realized she had postpartum depression. "I felt like I could finally breathe again," she said. "Like someone 'had' me, was helping me carry this load. My therapist helped me see how hard I was being on myself, and the kind way she spoke to me became more the way I spoke to myself. She helped me feel hopeful."

One study showed that depression scores over the year after giving birth were higher when the mothers had a larger overall workload (paid and unpaid labor), less job flexibility, less social support, and a baby with sleep issues.[14] This shows the importance of some of these factors in our mood after giving birth. Paying more attention to our workload, job expectations, social support, and sleep can help when we're feeling low. While some of these factors may be out of our control, we can still do certain things to adjust or adapt our schedules or reach out to friends more often.

POSTPARTUM ANXIETY

Here are the symptoms of postpartum anxiety:

- Worried thoughts that feel constant, excessive, or out of control
- Racing thoughts
- Feelings of dread, as if something bad is going to happen
- Unusual irritability
- Difficulty with sleeping or appetite due to worry
- Restlessness or difficulty with sitting still or concentrating due to worry thoughts
- Physical symptoms such as nausea, dizziness, heart palpitations, and panic attacks[15]

It's normal to feel worried about your baby. What we're talking about with postpartum anxiety is a more excessive and longer-lasting type of worry—one that feels like the level of worry is affecting your well-being and mental health. Anxiety is the most common mental health diagnosis in the general population. Over 30 percent of adults in the US will have an anxiety disorder at some time in their lives.[16] Because you have so many new things to worry about once you've had a baby, there is a high likelihood that any amount of anxiety you already experience will be heightened. It's also likely that the actual diagnosis rates of postpartum anxiety are much lower than they should be, since so many new moms "explain away" their worry or think it must be normal. The key is to identify if the amount of anxiety feels like too much *to you* or if it's impacting your life in ways you don't like. These are the signs that you may want to get professional help.

OTHER POSTPARTUM MENTAL HEALTH CONDITIONS

Other mental health concerns might come up after you have a baby that are still important to address right away if you notice them. For example, some women develop obsessive-compulsive symptoms during pregnancy or after giving birth. This may include having intrusive images or thoughts about your baby and sometimes performing rituals or compulsive behaviors to reduce the anxiety.

Post-traumatic stress disorder (PTSD) can also develop during pregnancy or after having a baby. For instance, you may have had a traumatic birth experience that has led you to experience flashbacks or nightmares, increased anxiety or panic, detachment, or avoidance of things that remind you of the birth. Or you may have had a completely normal birth experience that triggered memories of past trauma such as sexual assault or rape, abuse, or frightening medical situations. Dealing with trauma often requires professional help, because it's more than just convincing ourselves to not think about something that happened in the past. Psychological or physical trauma causes changes to the parts of our brain's limbic system that are in charge of memories, emotions, and self-regulation; and it often takes conscious and guided work to help heal and recover these processes after traumatic events.[17]

Bipolar disorders, in which you experience major depressive episodes as well as manic episodes where you may feel extremely agitated, euphoric, impulsive, and/or driven, can also occur during the postpartum period. Postpartum psychosis, in which a mother experiences delusional thinking or breaking with reality, hallucinations (seeing or hearing things that are not real), or paranoia, is rare but more serious.[18] As with PTSD, these conditions likely require help from a mental health professional.

It's important to know that if you have any of the symptoms discussed above, *it absolutely does NOT mean that you're a bad mother.* Even good moms have out-of-control thoughts or feelings sometimes, and the fact that you might have such thoughts and feelings doesn't define you as a mother. You're so much more than a thought that pops into your head or a feeling you have. Sometimes mothers think that if they have a terrible thought, either it's likely to happen or they might do something terrible. The truth is that these thoughts that come into your head aren't within your control, but how you respond to them is. A mental health professional will absolutely help you sort out the thoughts from reality and work with you on any fears that something is wrong with you. If this is a big point of worry for you, you may want to check out Karen Kleiman's book *Good Moms Have Scary Thoughts.*

WHAT TO DO ABOUT POSTPARTUM MENTAL HEALTH CONCERNS

If you experience any of these symptoms for longer than you'd like, it can be helpful to reach out to a therapist who has experience or training in postpartum mental health. You can start by visiting the PSI website (www.postpartum.net) and searching through their online provider directory.

Getting help for a mental health issue, especially one related to your birth or postpartum concerns, isn't a sign of weakness. Going to therapy is becoming more accepted and even expected, and it can help solve several of the issues you may be dealing with postpartum. Therapy can offer professional social support, help with self-esteem and feelings of competence as a new mother, and show you how normal your fears and struggles are. Therapy gives you a sounding board and insight that you might not otherwise have. There is only so much we can do on our own without input. If you hit a point where it becomes difficult to move through your feelings for whatever reason, that might be where a therapist or professional can help. A therapist—as opposed to your sister, mother, or partner—is trained to be objective, nonjudgmental, and focused on *you*, which is a perspective few other people in your life can offer.

PRACTICE: *Changing Your Negative Thoughts to Positive Affirmations*

If you're struggling with postpartum depression, recall the feeling of love openness and acceptance that you cultivated earlier in this book. Bring it back to your mind and body. Let it shine on the part of you that feels depressed or sad. Don't try to change this part of you. Instead, view it through the lens of acceptance and love.

Next, from this more open and accepting light, see if you've been believing harsh or negative things about yourself. Write them down if you can identify them.

Think about why you believe them and whether it would feel better to challenge them or put your energy into believing their opposites. Consider how it would feel to let go of those negative thoughts. For example, would it be freeing? Would it make you feel lighter?

If some thoughts or beliefs feel harder to let go, write down the exact opposite of each negative thought. For example, if you identified that you're thinking *I am a terrible mother*, write down *I am a great/fantastic/awesome/wonderful mother*. Choose a word that resonates with you as the exact opposite of your original thought.

Take a few moments to repeat and breathe in each of the opposite statements that you wrote. These are the affirmations that you need to hear most! So breathe them in. Feel what it's like to believe them.

This is a practice of changing your thinking in a way that is more helpful to you. If you don't believe the opposite statements or affirmations right now, that's okay. Use this exercise to repeat them and breathe them in every day, and see if it becomes easier to believe them over time.

If depression and negative thinking are some of your main challenges, you may find Karen Kleiman and Valerie Davis Raskin's book, *This Isn't What I Expected: Overcoming Postpartum Depression*, helpful.

PRACTICE: *Calming Your Anxiety and Challenging Your Worries*

If you struggle with postpartum anxiety, pay attention to when your anxiety rises. Identify any relaxation tools that have worked for you in the past: deep breathing, yoga, walking, spending time outdoors, cuddling your baby or a pet, listening to music, etc. Practice these relaxation tools first.

When you feel calmer and better able to think, identify what was making you anxious. Can you pinpoint a specific fear or worry? If so, consider how you can challenge that anxiety-producing thought. Is it possible you're overestimating the probability that something bad will happen? Or that you're assuming the worst possible outcome and maybe making the situation worse than it actually is?

Next, think about what you need from yourself to challenge that thought and try a different one. It could be a thought such as *I'm exaggerating how bad this is* or *My baby and I are fine* or an affirmation such as *I am doing my best* or *I'm keeping my baby and myself safe.* Whatever the soothing thought may be, take some deep breaths while repeating it to yourself.

Focus on this message, and breathe it in and out to calm your nerves and your heart.

If you find that postpartum anxiety is an issue for you, you may want to look into *The Pregnancy & Postpartum Anxiety Workbook* by Pamela S. Wiegartz and Kevin L. Gyoerkoe.

In all of these hard things that you have done, are doing, and will do, what is most important is that you hold on to your sense of self-compassion.[19] If you're doing your best in everything you do, you are doing enough—and you're doing the right thing. How you feel about yourself through all of these hard things matters so much, because you are your strongest supporter (and also your toughest critic). Kristin Neff has done extensive research on self-compassion and consistently finds that we tend to be much easier on others than we are on ourselves.[20] This can be helpful when considering how to shift out of our usual or "autopilot" thinking about ourselves. For example, we can frame our thoughts about ourselves to mirror what we would say to a friend in a similar situation.

PRACTICE: *Giving Yourself the Gift of Self-Compassion*

Think about a situation that's hard for you right now. Recognize that what you're feeling is suffering, in some sense. Gently tell yourself that you recognize that you're suffering and that many people are suffering or have suffered in similar ways.

Next, consider what you would say to a good friend if they were feeling the way you're feeling. Put into words and even physical gestures what you would offer your friend. Then say and do these things for yourself. In other words, say what you'd say to a friend to yourself, and give yourself a hug or another gesture of affection if that's what you would offer them.

It may be helpful to write down what you'd say to a friend who is going through something hard. This is likely something you need to hear more often for yourself. If you do write it down, keep it somewhere you'll look at it when you need to remind yourself of those words.

Being a new mom is full of hard things. It can be difficult to see beyond them sometimes, but it's helpful to keep your eye on the bigger goal and purpose: to get through these times and hold on to your love for your baby and for yourself. If we remind ourselves of this every day, then the hard things might become just things—tasks we have to do that we trust we *can* do.

CHAPTER 4 CHECKLIST

Here are the practices you learned in this chapter:

1. Inhaling Self-Acceptance and Exhaling Willingness
2. Letting Go of Expectations
3. Focusing on Your Strengths
4. Finding Your Maternal Instinct
5. Listening to Your Maternal Instinct
6. Recognizing Your Part in a Relationship Conflict
7. Communicating Using Assertive Language
8. Keeping the Team Together
9. Accepting the Things You Can't Control
10. Allowing for Flexibility as You Go Back to Work
11. Changing Your Negative Thoughts to Positive Affirmations
12. Calming Your Anxiety and Challenging Your Worries
13. Giving Yourself the Gift of Self-Compassion

Pick two favorites from the list above. Write them on a piece of paper and tape it to your bathroom mirror. Make the practices that were useful to you a part of your daily routine, and consider marking the ones that were harder to connect with so you can explore them further or try them again later. Practice doesn't make perfect, but it helps to make it a habit and deepen the positive effects the more you try these exercises.

5

Releasing Your Fear:

From
"I'm Scared"
to
"I Am Brave and Capable"

IF YOU'RE DOUBTING YOUR TOUGHNESS, let me tell you this: Moms are the toughest people on this planet. We've endured the process of growing an entire person inside of us, birthing that baby into the world, and then keeping it alive, all with little sleep, rest, and other essential human resources. Whether your pregnancy was planned or your birth went smoothly, the fact that you brought a baby into the world is a brave and hopeful act. That perspective is important to hold on to through the hard times to come, no matter how difficult it may seem. Our attention is pulled in so many directions with a newborn baby, so it's easy to lose sight of the fact that even though we may have chosen this, and really wanted this, we weren't fully prepared for what having it means.

Doing the hard things is a feat. But how you *feel* about how you're doing is just as (if not more) important. Tapping into your strengths and building confidence can help you feel as though you've got this—and you've definitely got this! It's just hard to keep up that feeling at times when life isn't going the way you expected or planned.

PRACTICE: *Owning Your Strengths*

Think about things that you know are strengths of yours. What are some characteristics that other people—family members, friends, bosses, coworkers, partners, teachers, etc.—have praised you for in the past? Consider the things you know you're pretty good at, regardless of those qualifiers you might usually tell yourself because your brain wants to downplay what makes you unique and wonderful (e.g., "Someone else does it better" or "Yeah, but . . .").

Write down the strengths you see in yourself or that you've heard from others. Aim for at least three strengths.

Look at this list, and state each characteristic as an "I am . . ." statement. For instance, you may have written down *organized* as a strength, so write out or say, "I am organized." This becomes an affirmation, something that is true about you and can be helpful to say out loud or see in writing when you doubt yourself or can't identify any of the strengths you have within you.

If you have a hard time believing any of the strengths you've listed (even though others have said them about you), or if you know you need to remind yourself of your strengths often, write them on a Post-it Note or dry-erase board or mirror you can look at often. When you see the words first thing in the morning or frequently throughout the day, say them out loud to yourself. Maybe even look at yourself in the mirror and smile while you say them. With affirmations, repetition is key! That way, you can re-record the thoughts in your mind to be positive ones that allow you to focus on your strengths.

AFFIRMING YOUR STRENGTHS

We all have strengths! We all have weaknesses as well. We're just more tuned in to those weaknesses than to our strengths. Developing a stronger awareness of our strengths is a skill we need to build ourselves so that we can feel good about who we are and our ability to handle things that come at us. The practice of focusing our minds on our strengths helps us create a more positive inner voice than the one we might be used to. Many of us live with negative self-talk, a running commentary in our minds of all of the things that we've done wrong or that we think make us terrible at something. This is pretty debilitating if you want to feel good about yourself or if you're making changes in your life. So change the channel. Create affirming messages that are as loud and audible as the negative thoughts, and repeat them as often as you hear those doubting messages in your head.

SAMPLE AFFIRMATIONS

If a Common Thought for You is . . .	Try Repeating This to Yourself Instead
"I'm a bad mother." (This includes any variation of the thought, such as "So-and-so is much better at this than I am.")	"I am doing the best I can, and loving my child makes me the best mom for them."
"I can't do this anymore."	"I need a break, and I deserve to take one."
"Something bad is going to happen."	"I am doing my best to take care of my baby and we are safe."
"I have to do everything myself."	"I deserve to ask for help and let others help me."
"My baby's crying, which means I'm doing something wrong."	"Babies cry. I am still learning about my baby and I am doing the best I can to help them. And I need and deserve a break sometimes."

Research says that partner or parent-child relationships are best when there is a five-to-one ratio of positive and negative interactions—that is, when there are about five positive or affirming exchanges for every negative one.[1,2] This is best for us as adults in our romantic relationships and also best for kids as we parent them (or as teachers instruct them) toward optimal development.[3] It's also pretty hard to give that amount of positivity to others if you can't give that ratio of positive affirmations to yourself. If your internal monologue is primarily negative, you'll have a hard time seeing and calling out the positive to anyone else. So start by noticing how often you say something negative or deprecating about yourself; and consciously, in that moment, think of five positive affirmations or strengths about yourself that you can call to mind to fight against that critical voice.

If you give yourself an especially hard time about your abilities as a parent, you'll first need to focus on identifying your strengths in the parenting realm—and you do have them! Sometimes it's hard to find them, especially when all of the hard things that happen make you feel like you're not great at this "mom job."

PRACTICE: *Focusing on Your Strengths as a Parent*

Reflect on the characteristics you associate with a "good parent" or "good mom." Write them down. Circle the ones that you feel you already have. Check your list of strengths to see if anything there applies.

Next, write out each of the characteristics you circled that make you a good parent. Write "I am . . ." and then the strength you have as a parent. Review and reflect on this list when you need help remembering that you already bring some strengths into this role.

There will be a million moments when you doubt that you're doing a good job. Remember that self-doubt is just a feeling, a signal for you to pay attention to something within. Doubting thoughts may signal to you that you need to spend time in your strengths, doing things you already feel good about. It also might be a sign that you need to show yourself some love, care, and affirmation.

You might not feel confident in knowing what you need when you have feelings like self-doubt. Here is where a practice called RAIN might come in handy. RAIN is an acronym that can help you sort through your feelings in a nonjudgmental way, then do something to take care of yourself in that feeling.

PRACTICE: *Using the RAIN Method*

If you feel unsettled or troubled and you're not sure why, take a few moments to turn inward and follow these steps:

R – Recognize what is going on inside of you. Think about what sensations you're feeling and where in your body you are feeling them. Notice what is happening for you, without trying to label or fix it.

A – Acknowledge that this feeling is real and a part of you right now. Practice acceptance toward the feeling, allowing it to be with you. You don't have to identify with it; just allow it.

I – Investigate with a gentle curiosity what the feeling might mean or be trying to tell you. What does it want you to know?

N – Nurture yourself by thinking about what would feel good, given this feeling that you're having. What kind of care do you want? If it is hard to figure out, consider what you would offer to a friend who is feeling this way. Then think about how you can give yourself that kind of care.

Getting in touch with your strengths and acknowledging your feelings of weakness will bring acceptance, which is one of your most powerful tools. There is also a lot of management in new motherhood—things you have to get through, whether you feel like you're good at them or not. So much of the exhaustion of parenthood is the sheer volume of tasks and things to keep in your mind every single day. Maybe you don't feel great about your ability to handle this management and infant care. Maybe you're extremely organized, and you enjoy this challenge. Or maybe you dread the amount of work there is to do each day and are overwhelmed by it. The goal doesn't have to be to change your personality so that you *love* doing laundry, changing poopy diapers, and keeping up with the feeding schedule. The goal can be as simple as feeling *capable* of managing it all.

The fact is, if you're managing all the responsibilities of a baby and those of your own life, you're doing great. There is no measure or marker for how well you're supposed to be at this balance. This means that "just doing it" is actually the goal—and you *are* doing it! Shifting your view of how you're "supposed to be" doing at managing things to "pass/fail" instead of a graded system is the first step toward seeing capability as ability, as well as appreciating yourself just for showing up.

The difference between the two words—*ability* and *capability*—is an interesting one. If you are *able* to do something, it means you *can* do it or that you have done it before. If you are *capable*, however, it means you have the potential to do it. The only difference is whether you do it. You are (and have always been) capable of being a mom, and right now you're building your ability to do it. So when you're on the other side, you can say that you know you can do it because you did it before! What a different way of viewing yourself, right? We are all building our abilities all the time, just by doing things. You are, right at this moment, building your mom abilities. Thinking of yourself in this light—that you are capable *and* able—highlights the power of just showing up. Even on the days you show up crying or having a breakdown, you're becoming more able.

PRACTICE: *Appreciating Yourself*

Take a few moments of quiet time to think about what you appreciate about yourself. This can be traits that you get praised for, like kindness, generosity, and thoughtfulness. Or they can be abilities such as being a good parent, friend, cook, or listener. If nothing else, appreciate the fact that you continue to show up. You are capable *and* able.

Reflect on these traits and abilities as being true about you, not with qualifiers or statements like, "If they only knew . . ." Instead, practice believing those qualities and feeling grateful and appreciative for them.

MAKING MEANING FROM HARD TIMES

Research shows that going through hard times builds our sense of *resilience*, or the ability to "bounce back," cope with, or positively adapt when things are difficult. Studies have shown that going through adversity or hard times gives you more resilience and better mental health and well-being than someone who never experiences adversity.[4] In addition, a beautiful study of mothers of very low-birth-weight babies in the NICU describes how a key piece of healing for these mothers was a shift from living in the loss and difficulty of the situation to finding meaning in the distress and growing from it.[5] This change in perspective is challenging but not outside of our control. When we're in the hard things, we can choose whether to sit in it or move forward.

That isn't to say we shouldn't give ourselves time to be sad, lonely, or exhausted. As we talked about earlier in this book, whatever you're feeling is okay, valid, and worth experiencing! In fact, allowing the feelings is an important part of the process of moving toward healing and resilience. It's just that, at some point, you have to start moving. Dwelling in feelings of overwhelm, anxiety, depression, and all the rest doesn't resolve them. The next part (when you're ready for it) is to pick up those feelings and start to walk with them—to continue on your journey with those feelings as a symbol of what you've been through, not as an anchor that keeps you there.

You may remember Anya from chapter 2, who lost her first baby and had high anxiety throughout her second pregnancy and the baby's infancy. Anya recognized after several months of agonizing worry about her second baby that it was up to *her* to shift her thinking. With the help of her therapist, Anya realized that her worry was keeping her from being fully present and loving with this second baby in all the ways she wanted to be. She worked to separate her worry, which was about another baby and another circumstance, from *this* baby and *this* time as a mother. Separating her two experiences as a new mother made Anya feel that she was more fully honoring her first baby's memory; she was allowing those feelings of fear and worry to be in the past and about that situation, instead of about the child she now held.

It can be helpful to visualize yourself making this transition in perspective, from sitting in your feelings to moving, especially during times when you feel stuck in resentment, overwhelm, or worrying or thinking about the same things all the time. When you can see that you're stuck, you can make the conscious decision to choose whether to continue on in your stuckness.

Who decides when it's time to move on? You do! No one else can decide for you when it's time to switch from being in your feelings to taking action or moving on. Sure, you may have people in your life who you trust to let you know when you're stuck and others who believe in tough love and will let you know whether you want to or not. But ultimately, it's your own choice and motivation that will drive you out of feelings of stuckness and into something more helpful.

PRACTICE: *Getting Yourself Unstuck*

When you feel stuck in a certain feeling or thought, first practice recognizing and accepting that feeling or thought, allowing it to be a part of you and acknowledging that it's important. You may need to spend several days or more in this phase of just acknowledging how you feel.

When you feel ready, think about what you need to move on from this stuckness and if you need to take any care to feel prepared to go. Maybe you need one last cry, a good night's sleep, encouragement from a friend or partner, or to just get yourself excited and pumped up for the next part of the journey.

Then, visualize yourself picking up your pack and moving again along your path. You aren't leaving your feelings or experiences behind; you're taking them with you, learning from them and allowing them to be a part of you as you go. Recognize yourself for the strength it takes to start moving again after something hard happens or after you've been stuck for some time. Remind yourself that this strength is something you carry with you as well and is there whenever you need it.

This shift toward seeing yourself as able to move through and with your feelings is important to your overall resilience the next time things are hard. It gets easier each time to adapt or move forward after adversity if you're able to accept the feelings that hard times cause and integrate them into your bigger picture or your life journey. Having gone through the struggle gives you skills and abilities that you might not have otherwise had. Research calls this "resilient reintegration" when some kind of disruption to your "norm" leads you to gain protective factors that ultimately make you better off than you were before the disruption.[6]

But why would we be better off going through hard things? There are a number of reasons. First, the hard things make us tap into our strengths and resources (including connecting to our social support), build up our ability to protect ourselves in the face of harm, and feel a sense of mastery that we might not have had before.[7] We've talked about ways to call your strengths to mind and get the social support you need. It's also worth reflecting on how good it feels to conquer difficult situations. These positive aspects of ourselves are easy to skim over when we are in survival mode and just facing or getting through one hard thing after another.

PRACTICE: *Celebrating Your Resilience*

When you're at the end of a difficulty—no matter if it's your baby finally falling asleep after a seemingly never-ending crying spell, you getting to the end of a day where you didn't have time to shower or talk to another adult, or you discussing a tricky subject with your partner—take a moment to congratulate and celebrate yourself. Tell yourself, "Good job, you made it," and find a way to commend or enjoy yourself. Remind yourself that you deserve a celebration after what you went through. It could be a shower, a hot cup of tea, a little dance party, or an actual round of applause or hug for yourself—any kind of reminder that you're stronger and more masterful because of every single hard thing you've gone through.

You may even want to plan the celebration while you're in the middle of the hard thing. Think about how good that shower will feel after your baby falls asleep or how wonderful it will feel to listen to that empowering music or throw yourself that little party after the tough conversation. Having these rewards to look forward to makes it easier to get through the challenges and makes you more attuned to the positive things you can do for yourself.

The second important piece of building resilience is maintaining (or regaining) perspective. This means seeing difficult times for what they are, as temporary—no matter if it's a long period of your baby not sleeping well or encountering a medical issue—and knowing that they'll pass. You can also hold them as meaningful without staying stuck in them. This sometimes means "stepping outside" of yourself and the experience of the moment to see what is beautiful, unique, or even humorous about what is happening. It helps to think outside of the feeling you might be having at that moment, whether you're exhausted from not sleeping or struggling to see that you are teaching your baby self-soothing skills that will help them for the rest of their lives. It also helps to laugh at yourself when you're so tired that you mismatch your shoes. These are the memories that will endear this difficult phase to you down the road.

Keeping perspective or making meaning also means seeing all of the hard things of motherhood—the tasks and "management" that come with keeping a baby alive and a home functioning—in perspective. For you, it may mean letting go of things that aren't as important (like cleaning the bathroom or doing the dishes) without feeling bad or judging yourself for it. It may also mean finding meaning in the "meaningless" or mundane tasks you have to do each day. Thinking about why you do these tasks can help ease the frustration or resentment you might feel about having to do them. For example, instead of thinking, *I have to wash so many damn bottles all the time*, try thinking, *Washing these bottles reminds me how grateful I am to have a healthy baby who has enough to eat.* Or instead of thinking, *It's so much work to shop and prep our food for the week*, it might feel more fulfilling to think, *I am taking such good care of myself and my family by working this hard.*

PRACTICE: *Creating Meaning from Your Routine*

Choose one activity you have to do today as part of taking care of your baby. Allow yourself to be fully present while you're doing this task, and consider how meaningful it is. Whether you're washing bottles, doing laundry, or cleaning the house, think to yourself, *I am taking care of my baby and my family by doing this.* Reflect on how this feels. Write about your experience.

Remind yourself daily (if not more) how brave and capable you are by doing what you're doing. As we talked about earlier in this chapter, each time you say something positive to yourself or call your strengths to mind—and hopefully you're recognizing that you have many—you'll fill your emotional tank a little more. This will help you carry or put down your burdens, hold on through the hard things, and shift toward acceptance and maybe even joy in just how wonderfully well you're doing.

CHAPTER 5 CHECKLIST

Here are the practices you learned in this chapter:

1. Owning Your Strengths
2. Focusing on Your Strengths as a Parent
3. Using the RAIN Method
4. Appreciating Yourself
5. Getting Yourself Unstuck
6. Celebrating Your Resilience
7. Creating Meaning from Your Routine

Pick two favorites from the list above. Write them on a piece of paper and tape it to your bathroom mirror. Make the practices that were useful to you a part of your daily routine, and consider marking the ones that were harder to connect with so you can explore them further or try them again later. Practice doesn't make perfect, but it helps to make it a habit and deepen the positive effects the more you try these exercises.

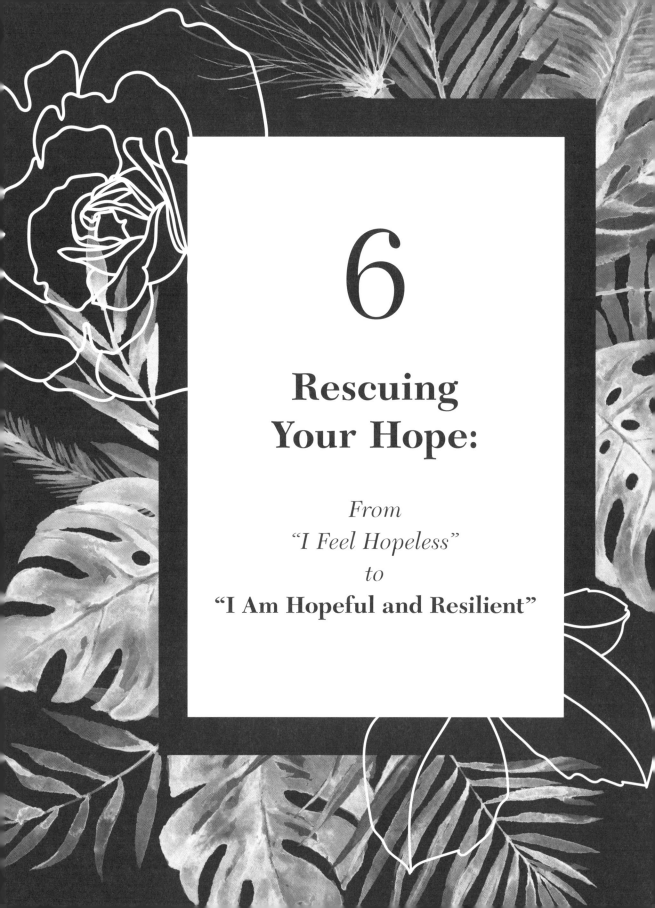

6

Rescuing Your Hope:

From
"I Feel Hopeless"
to
"I Am Hopeful and Resilient"

HOPE IS ONE OF THE MOST POWERFUL emotions because it's the one that most motivates change and growth. Think about it: you're not likely to work toward getting better at something if you don't think it's possible!

Hope is about focusing on the possibilities. This is a practice, too, like so many things you've practiced in this book. So let's talk about practicing the cultivation of hope. This is a big skill, because there will be times when you won't have hope in the forefront of your mind and you may be more focused on the barriers and what is going wrong than the possibilities. Like with any positive feeling, we want to call the feeling of hope to mind when we need it. This is like building muscle memory. When you practice something physically, your body learns it and then remembers how it felt, so that it's easier to do the next time.

PRACTICE: *Building Emotional Muscle Memory*

Bring to mind something you have hope for or are hopeful about. It can be something simple, such as your baby taking a good nap. Or it can be something more complicated, such as hoping your child will turn out to be a caring, thoughtful person. Hold the thought of possibility that this will happen in your mind. Set aside any doubts or negative thoughts about this for another time. Right now, you're focusing on the hope and possibility that what you wish for will happen. Feel what hope feels like in your body. Maybe it's a lightness in your chest or a flutter or tingle of excitement. Focus on the positive feelings about the unknown. Hold this feeling for as long as you can.

Write down some of the things that will help you bring this feeling back to mind when you're feeling down or hopeless:

Hope is an important choice to make consciously. Very often we're motivated by fear—maybe without even recognizing it. Maybe you go online to research how and when to introduce certain foods to your baby and come across several pages with good information and plans, then read a comment in which someone says their baby had an awful allergic reaction after eating a certain food. This one comment is likely to hook your attention more than the factual information, because it hits on the fears that we all have. The activation of that fear can change the whole course of your research; and you might go down a rabbit hole either figuring out what to do to minimize your baby's risk or getting discouraged and putting it off altogether.

Fear is a powerful motivator. In fact, it is the most powerful thing that stops us from doing things. However, it's not the ultimate in motivation. What actually motivates us to *take* action is positive reinforcement—recognition, hope, a desire to improve, and the belief that you can.[1] So the way to counteract fear or immobility isn't with more fear, since that would ultimately paralyze you. Instead, the way to fight fear is with hope. Which one feels better to you?

Here are times when fear can play a role, whether you recognize it or not:

- You read about something terrible that happened to someone else or their baby.
- Your baby isn't feeling well or is going through a tough stage, and you don't know what to do.
- You think there is a right or wrong way to do something, product to buy, way to parent, etc.
- You have fears about having an accident, something or someone harming your child, or other events you can't control.
- You compare yourself to others and feel like you don't "measure up."
- You feel alone or unsupported.
- You focus on what you don't have or what you lack.
- You think that whatever hard stage or feeling is happening right now will last forever.

In any of these situations, focusing on the fear only serves to make you feel more scared and incapable. Fear makes us feel despair and helplessness, and it tells us we can't—we can't stop, can't prevent, can't do enough, can't get through, and so on. But the thing is, we can't live in *can't*. It doesn't tell us what to do but rather what we aren't able or supposed to do.

Hope helps us overcome this feeling of paralysis because it depends on two things. First, we can *want for something better* and also believe that we can *do something* to help us to get there.[2] Practicing hope also builds self-confidence that you can do something to make positive changes or feel better. It's a two-for-one benefit that way: we can feel more hopeful and also more confident in our ability to handle things.

PRACTICE: *Turning from Fear toward Hope*

When you feel anxious about something or recognize that there is a powerful fear message coming at you (e.g., any of the things on the list on the previous page), take a break for a purposeful hope practice.

First, bring to mind how you hope the situation will turn out, everything you know about what is likely to happen, and what is likely to change and/or improve. Remember that this is just a phase and won't last forever. Activate your rational brain to calm and soothe the emotions that are brought up by fear. Focus on your feeling of hope for how this will turn out.

Next, call to mind an image of you as a confident person who can handle this situation. Feel your own power coursing through you. Recognize that this power is within you all the time and can be called upon when you need it. If an image or word pops up when you think of yourself this way, use it as your own keyword, a way to visually and powerfully recall your confident and able self when you need her.

Write down any words or images that help you recapture this version of yourself:

....

....

....

....

....

....

REFRAMING

When you pivot your thinking from fear to hope (or from any negative thought toward a more positive one), you're practicing the magic of reframing—changing your perspective slightly to see things differently. It's like shifting the picture frame to see a different part of the image. That may mean focusing in to see a beautiful detail you miss when you're looking at the whole picture or zooming out to see beyond the tiny pixels to the full sunset.

One new mom I know was so anxious about her baby's cognitive development that she would research every stage ahead of time, plan for stimulating activities to keep baby on track, and fill her home with books and educational toys designed to encourage age-appropriate learning. When I said to her, "You're his mom, not his teacher," she reeled at the fact that she was putting so much pressure on herself to teach her baby's brain instead of just caring for his soul and loving him to the best of her ability. This reframing helped her put her energy into the things that made her the best mom for her baby and less into worrying about his learning.

Reframing is magical because it can be a very small shift in thinking. It's not about changing the facts of the situation at all but about viewing them slightly differently. This can mean the difference between believing that nothing you do is good enough and thinking of your willingness to keep trying as a strength. Another new mom I know was so worried that she or her baby were going to get sick that she spent a lot of time researching various illnesses on the internet. This didn't make her feel better, but rather much worse and more anxious. An important reframing moment came when she realized that the time she was spending on WebMD and worrying about what could happen to her or her baby was actually causing her to miss the beautiful moments she was having with her healthy baby. Seeing how this worry distracted her from what was important gave her a cue to follow: whenever she felt worried that she or her baby would get sick, she would tune in, pay extra care and attention to her baby, and enjoy each moment—even the moments when her baby had a runny nose or a nasty diaper.

Reframing can come in the form of thinking, *Maybe I am meant to learn something from this. What could it be?*

Looking for a lesson or meaning in a difficult situation can help you reframe something that could feel awful into something more helpful. One new mom felt socially isolated and knew that she needed connection, but she felt so awkward starting a conversation with another mom in her mom-child classes or at her pediatrician's office that she held herself back from introducing herself to others. When she thought about what she feared would happen, she realized that "no one has ever died from being awkward," which helped her move through her fears and dive in. Making friends became much easier than she expected after that.

In therapy, the moment a client figures out a more helpful way of seeing the situation, she often experiences the biggest aha moment and turning point. Some of my clients will call out "REFRAME!" when they realize they can do this trick on their own. If you practice reframing consciously when you're feeling stuck or in a negative place, it becomes easier to reframe things naturally. Recognizing that there are multiple ways to view a situation and that you can just *choose* a more helpful view is powerful.

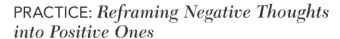

PRACTICE: *Reframing Negative Thoughts into Positive Ones*

When you find yourself dwelling on a negative or unhelpful thought about yourself or your abilities as a parent, see how you can practice your reframing skills.

First, consider what it would feel like to believe the opposite of your current thought. For example, if your negative thought is *I'm a bad mom because I'm so impatient*, try thinking *I'm a good mom because of my impatience.*

If that doesn't fit exactly, consider whether your thought contains any judgment words that can be swapped for less judgmental ones. Here are some examples:

Instead of *a bad mom*, think *an okay mom* or *a good enough mom.*

Instead of *impatient*, maybe you're *sensitive*, *eager*, or *efficient.*

Finally, think about whether there is a lesson in changing your way of thinking or whether you're able to broaden your view. To build on the examples used so far, you might think, *I want to work on being more patient. I am a good mom even though I have things to work on.*

Write down a statement that counteracts each negative thought. For instance, if you thought *I am a bad mom*, write down something true and positive about your abilities, like *I am doing my best as a mom because I keep trying even when it feels hard*. Repeat the positive statements to yourself, and bring them to mind when you find yourself having those negative thoughts.

Practice holding these more helpful thoughts or using them to pivot your thinking whenever old negative ones are running through your mind.

rescuing your hope

One helpful way to reframe someone else's behavior is to catch yourself when you find you're thinking that the other person *won't* do something, then see what happens when you swap out that *won't* with *can't*. What if, instead of thinking that your partner *won't* do their share of the baby care, you were to try out the idea that they *can't* do what you're expecting from them, either because they don't know to do it (i.e., if you haven't asked them directly) or they don't know how (if they've never been taught to do what you're expecting of them)? Reframing *won't* into *can't* places less blame on someone and puts you in a more constructive mindset about how you can help them learn what to do or how. If your partner can't do what you're asking because they don't know how, have never been shown how to do it, or didn't grow up in a family where the partner helped, this mindset allows you to ask questions, get your partner's perspective, and show or teach them skills they might not already have. These are all actions that build the feeling of teamwork and togetherness, rather than feelings of blame and resentment.

HOPE FOR PESSIMISTS

Reframing or focusing on hope isn't about becoming an optimist, especially if you don't feel that you are one naturally. Optimism is about expecting positive things in the future, so it's probably a more hopeful perspective than pessimism or the expectation of negative experiences happening.[3] However, you *can* be hopeful even if you're more of a pessimist!

In his book *Learned Optimism*, Martin Seligman talks about pessimism as a form of learned helplessness. People who have a more pessimistic view of the world often have learned it through life events; the way they were parented; or maybe even trauma, oppression, or discrimination. They put more mental emphasis on the things they can't control, so everything seems helpless. This frame of mind reinforces itself. If everything seems out of your control and you think that nothing you do matters, you're likely to not take any action to change the situation—and the situation will, in fact, stay the same. This makes optimism/pessimism more of a learned way of thinking than a natural tendency or trait that some people are born with.[4]

The field of positive psychology is based on this idea. If where you focus your mental energy influences how you feel, then choosing to focus more energy on the positive instead of the negative will help you feel better. This was a pretty radical shift in that field of science. Psychology was developed basically to tell us (women, especially) all the things that were wrong with us; and in a lot of ways, it was set up as a system that profited by keeping people sick. Not a lot of work was done to help us learn how to feel better. (Talk about setting people up for learned helplessness.) So positive psychology arose as a reframe: what if we focused more on what makes people feel better and what is right about (not wrong with) them and helped them through that lens instead of the old one?

For us personally, focusing on the positives in life—the good feelings, the happy moments, the things that bring us joy—has a lot of benefits. There is evidence that a positive perspective is associated with more subjective well-being (i.e., feeling better about our lives), resilience and ability to cope with difficult situations (which we covered in chapter 5), self-esteem, creativity, and potentially better overall health and a longer life.[5]

Some of the controversy around positive psychology is that positive thinking isn't enough to make everything go well. A lot of contextual factors also play into it. Some people believe that focusing on the positive is another reflection of privilege—in other words, that some people have a choice or opportunity to focus on the positive while others might not. For instance, a woman in an abusive relationship shouldn't feel responsible for focusing on the positive to make her life better. Nor should someone who is oppressed because of the color of their skin hold this obligation. Others may say that positive thinking is the same as ignoring the negative aspects of a situation, which might not be realistic or in your best interest. If there is a tiger in the woods and you're focused on the beautiful flowers, that tiger is probably going to eat you.

These points are all valid. Things can and will be bad sometimes. It isn't helpful to ignore or deny the hard things and only focus on the positives. I see the ability to pivot from fear toward hope as a skill that can be learned, not an optimistic outlook that some people have and others don't. Something we can all do is choose how we interpret negative circumstances. Whether we think that bad things happen because we must be bad people or that bad things "always" happen to us is another form of judgment. It doesn't help us to cope with those hard things. We can choose—and maybe get better at— seeing hard things as not personal, not intrinsic to us, and temporary instead of permanent. This helps us see those difficulties as bumps in the road and not defining, debilitating reasons to break down altogether.

Let's go back to *Learned Optimism* for a moment. In this book, Seligman also talks about the value of viewing negative circumstances as unlucky situations that aren't personal or permanent in nature but instead "finding temporary and specific causes of misfortune." This interpretation of things makes the difficult situation something we can deal with, not something to live with.[6] If our pessimism has been a habit for a long time, we need to identify how we're interpreting hard situations so that we can see how we can reshape or reframe our perspective on challenges.

PRACTICE: *Cultivating Hope Instead of Pessimism*

If you tend to expect that things will not go well, that bad things will happen to you in the future, or that others will not respond well when you bring up tough topics, catch yourself in one of these moments or thoughts. Recognize that you're expecting the worst or focusing on the worst part of something. Then consider whether you might be taking something personally and whether that's necessary. Are you seeing something as permanent when it just might be temporary or changeable? Are you allowing yourself to see others and events as they are? Or is there a voice in your head saying "Yeah, but . . ." and trying to convince you that the negative interpretation is the right one?

If you're hearing that voice in your head, ask it to step aside for a moment. Allow yourself to feel that what is happening might not be personal or terrible and that it may be temporary or changing in the future. Recall the feelings of openness and hopefulness that you practiced earlier (see pages 9 and 126), and take another look at the situation through this lens. Bring to mind a more objective, impersonal, and/or open-minded interpretation of things; and allow yourself to believe that interpretation. Breathe in and out through this different view of the situation, and reflect on how you feel.

FINDING EVIDENCE FOR YOUR STORY

You'll usually find what you're looking for. This is good news if you're searching for your keys or phone. But this also happens when we create internal stories about what is happening—and we do this a lot. If I think that my partner doesn't appreciate me or help me enough, I can find evidence to support that story. Each time my partner doesn't jump in to help clean up or doesn't say thank you, I can add that to the evidence that my story is correct. I might even feel some vindication when I notice these things, even though they aren't what I want my partner to do. This is a way that we reinforce our own thinking; we pay extra attention to anything that supports it, and we might glide right past anything that doesn't.

If you recognize that you're doing this, you can take back some control over it. You might be thinking, *Why would I want to change my story? It might be true!* It might be true that my partner doesn't help or appreciate me enough. But the thing is, holding onto and finding evidence for this story isn't helpful. In fact, it's pretty aggravating to me, and it probably creates a lot of tension between me and my partner that doesn't help the quality of our relationship. If I feel worn down and resentful by the story I'm holding onto, it may be more helpful for me to find evidence for the other side of the story—or even a new story.

How do we start? By identifying the story that we're telling ourselves. It often has to do with being put down or treated poorly by others. It may even have to do with feeling like we deserve to be treated this way. If I think that I'm a terrible mother and that I don't deserve appreciation, I'm going to find evidence for that story as well. Stepping outside of our internal monologue to see it more objectively lets us know what we're paying the most attention to. Then we can decide whether we want to keep supporting that story.

What would happen if we flipped the story—for example, thinking your partner is helping and appreciating you or that you're a good mother and deserve to be appreciated—and look for evidence of that? If we turn our attention to the things we do well or the encouragement our partner offers, we may find just as much evidence for these stories as for our original ones. It will also make us feel better to gather this kind of evidence and believe these stories.

PRACTICE: *Finding Evidence for a More Helpful Story*

Notice what kind of story you might be telling yourself about how you're feeling or being treated. It might be "I do the majority of the work around here" or "Nobody understands how hard this is." Think about whether you've been gathering evidence for this story.

Then, consider what it might feel like to flip this story. If you use the examples above, the more helpful versions would be "My partner and I each do the things we're good at" or "There are people in my life who understand how hard this is." Find evidence for your new story, and make note of the times when you feel this more helpful story is true. Notice if your perspective changes on what the "truth" might be and how you can find an interpretation that is more helpful or feels better to you.

If you can't find evidence for a more helpful story—for example, if your partner really doesn't help or appreciate you very often—this exercise may give you more useful language to talk about that with them. Remember the two most motivating components of hope: your vision of something getting better and your belief that you can do something to make that happen. These can be helpful pieces to think through as you prepare to talk to someone about a change you're hoping to see in your relationship with them.

PRACTICE: *Communicating Out of Hope*

If you want to improve or heal a relationship you have with another person, put yourself in a hopeful state of mind about it as you prepare to talk with them about it. First, imagine what you hope will happen between the two of you. Think about what you hope it will feel and look like. Why do you hope for this? What will it mean to you if it can happen?

Next, think about a step you can take to make your hopeful vision a reality. For example, if you imagined yourself talking more regularly with the other person, maybe you can make the first call and tell them, "I really hope we can talk more often, and I'm willing to do my part." Or if you imagined that your partner would show you more appreciation, you can ask them for a specific way they can recognize you and let them know why it's important to you (e.g., "I would love it if you could say thank you when you notice that I've cleaned up the house. It would make me feel like what I'm working hard on makes a difference to you.").

Then, consider what you hope to communicate to the other person and take that first step. If it doesn't go the way you wanted it to or they don't follow through, at least recognize that you did what you could to change the relationship in a small way.

REFRAMING MOM GUILT

As you work on finding joy and hope and reframing negative thoughts and fear, you may experience an increase in your feelings of mom guilt, or the guilt we feel as mothers when we need or want time away from our children. This is a common theme for mothers. An old message underlies this type of guilt: that mothers should live in service to their children and be gratified by this role alone, and that they shouldn't need time away or for themselves— ever. Because of this old message, some of us feel guilty if we look forward to going back to work or ask for an afternoon off for self-care.

Mom guilt also arises when you feel like you aren't doing "enough" for your kids or aren't a "good" mom. By now, hopefully you recognize that the voice of your mom guilt is full of judgments and fears—fears that you can't live up to an unreasonable, unrealistic standard of how moms "should" be. But how ridiculous is it to think moms "should" only ever be a certain way? Remember to flag words such as *should* in your mind as judgmental, unhelpful ideas that need to be examined and replaced with more helpful, strength-based, motivating beliefs.

Messages like this create fear in us that what we're doing is wrong and will have horrible consequences down the road. The feeling of mom guilt tells us that we don't deserve to have time to ourselves, that we don't deserve a life outside of our baby or our role as a mother, and that we shouldn't be happy away from our baby. Well, our new message is that we get to have a self outside of our baby and our role of motherhood and that not only do we deserve that self, we also need it.

PRACTICE: *Reframing Your Sense of Mom Guilt*

When you experience feelings of guilt related to parenting (e.g., you feel bad because you need or want a break away from your baby or family, or you feel like you're not doing enough as a mom), remind yourself that these feelings are signals for you to pay attention to something. Think about what the guilt may be pointing toward. Is it an old message you heard from someone else that you "shouldn't" need a break or "should" be doing something more? If so, reflect on whether this judgmental message is fair or true.

Next, consider whether you can give yourself a more helpful message. If you recognize one of those old messages, try out the opposite. For example, instead of saying, "I shouldn't need a break from my child," tell yourself "It's totally reasonable to want a break from my child. It's something I need to be the best mom I can be." Or instead of saying, "I should be doing more of _____ (e.g., playing with my baby, enjoying my baby, helping my baby learn)," tell yourself, "The amount of _____ I am doing is enough," or simply, "I am doing enough."

If you need one of these reframes more often, write it on a Post-it Note or ask a loved one to remind you of it. Make this a loving reminder to yourself when feelings of guilt pop up due to your old way of thinking.

Making a conscious and consistent effort to shift from fear to hope is important for another reason: it pulls us out of new-mom survival mode, where we're just doing what we can to keep ourselves and our family alive. Of course we're going to live in that mindset some of the time. We're new at this, arguably for the first several years; and even after that, we're new at each different stage and with each change, child, and interaction. So it's okay that sometimes we're just getting through it. However, it's important to remember that you *can* pull yourself out of survival mode when you want or need to, so that you can live and breathe in the present moment; enjoy this chaotic and full life; and hold on to feelings of joy, self-compassion, and hope about the future.

CHAPTER 6 CHECKLIST

Here are the practices you learned in this chapter:

1. Building Emotional Muscle Memory
2. Turning from Fear toward Hope
3. Reframing Negative Thoughts into Positive Ones
4. Cultivating Hope Instead of Pessimism
5. Finding Evidence for a More Helpful Story
6. Communicating Out of Hope
7. Reframing Your Sense of Mom Guilt

Pick two favorites from the list above. Write them on a piece of paper and tape it to your bathroom mirror. Make the practices that were useful to you a part of your daily routine, and consider marking the ones that were harder to connect with so you can explore them further or try them again later. Practice doesn't make perfect, but it helps to make it a habit and deepen the positive effects the more you try these exercises.

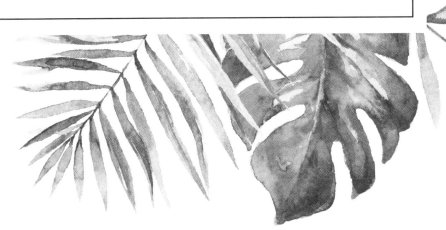

7

Owning Your Strength:

From
"I Am Weak"
to
"I Can Share My Strength with Others"

YOU KNOW FROM EXPERIENCE that it can be isolating and lonely as a new mom. Maybe you have a wonderful support system—and that's great! Maybe you know someone else who is going through it right now (or will be in the future) with less support. Can you bravely put yourself out there and pass on some of the hope and wisdom you've learned through your journey?

It can be hard to share parts of your own difficult story, but it can also be so important for another mom to hear it. Studies show that when we listen to someone else's story, our brains actually synchronize.[1] Mirror neurons in our brain connect us with what the other person is feeling or sharing so we feel it too.[2] This is incredibly important in feeling empathy for others or understanding what they're feeling. It's also soothing and reassuring when we hear someone else sharing something that we've felt ourselves. So if you've been through something hard (like early motherhood), the best thing you can do is share your story with someone else who may need to hear it. And if you're going through something hard (like new motherhood) right now, the best thing you can do is listen to someone else's experience of it. This means that there is a huge need out there for moms to share and listen to each other in supportive, nonjudgmental, bond-forming ways. And if each of us does our small part in reaching out, we can weave our stories together into a net to hold those who come after us.

CULTIVATING EMPATHY

Why is empathy so important? Brené Brown talks about empathy as the willingness "to be present with someone else's pain," which is both the "heart of connection" and the "antidote to shame."[3] Listening to someone else and having a deep understanding of what they are or were feeling allows you to more fully connect with that person and feel less shame about your own struggles. Empathy is connection based on shared feelings—not necessarily shared experiences but rather the feelings underneath. When we recognize either something we have felt in someone else's story or our story in what someone else is feeling, we can bond or relate to them on a heart or core level, not just a cognitive or "head" level.

Many women have told me that they feel they're empaths, or that they deeply feel what others are feeling. I know just as many who don't feel that empathy is something that they're especially good at. There is a sense out there that empathy is something you're either born with or not. But just like with optimism, empathy is a skill that you can get better at—and if you're already very (or "too") empathetic, it's a skill that you can practice having boundaries with as well.

Nursing scholar Theresa Wiseman has written about how to practice empathy as a skill by identifying what she calls the four "attributes" of empathy. First is the ability to take someone else's perspective or put yourself in their shoes, so to speak. This is more than just listening to someone's story; it's enabling yourself to imagine being in that experience, affected by all of the same things that affected the other person, and feeling how it might have felt to be there. Second is the ability to stay out of judgment. Practicing a nonjudgmental stance allows you to stay connected to what you're hearing, rather than distancing yourself from it by "othering" it; separating it from you as "not me"; or thinking of it as good or bad, right or wrong. Staying out of judgment keeps you connected to the other person's perspective, instead of filtering it through your own experience or opinions. The third attribute of empathy is the ability to understand the other person's feelings. This means allowing yourself to feel what they felt or what they're feeling right in the moment of telling you their story. The final attribute is the ability to communicate your understanding and allow the other person to know that you feel and understand it.[4] Each of these pieces of empathy might be a practice; you might do well with some parts but want to connect with others more fully.

Empathy is important if you're concerned about social justice, because understanding others' experiences and perspectives allows you to see how they experience prejudice or oppression, or how their needs have been overlooked by larger systems.[5] A part of feeling empathy is embracing some social responsibility in wanting to help where we can. So when we meet a mom who lives in poverty and learn more about how she got there and how it feels inescapable or like a hole that keeps getting deeper, we feel a responsibility to use our privilege or resources to help. This can mean donating money, giving the mom some direct assistance, helping her navigate the complicated systems to get the benefits she needs, or working within our own areas of influence to change systems to be more accessible and responsive to people like her. We need empathy for others to see the inequities. We have to see the unfairness to lift up other moms to really change how we're seen and supported.

Think about where empathy may be important in your life. Maybe you want to feel closer or more connected to your partner instead of getting lost in arguments about parenting or housework. In this case, empathy may look like doing your best to understand their views (on parenting, housework, or whatever the topic you can't seem to get on the same page about) on a deeper level, not in the middle of an argument. Maybe you want to make a new mom friend or ask for support from another mom in your family or group of friends, but you aren't sure whether you've had similar experiences—or if that even matters. Empathy can be a powerful basis for friendship and the kind of support we talked about back in chapter 3: someone who you can feel emotionally close to, feel reassured by, and share experiences and connection with.

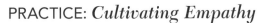

PRACTICE: *Cultivating Empathy*

If you're having trouble feeling empathy toward someone you want to feel more connected to (e.g., your partner, a family member, another mom), start by setting aside time and giving room to have a real, mindful conversation with that person. Minimize distractions as much as you can.

Next, see if you can begin a conversation in which you listen and do your best to take the other person's perspective. You could start by saying, "I want to understand more about your experience with . . ." Ask questions to help you understand what the other person is feeling, not to argue your perspective or try to solve anything. For instance, you could ask the other person, "What was that like? How did you feel about . . . ?" As they talk, imagine what they must be or have been feeling.

Then, recognize when you have judgmental thoughts (e.g., *They shouldn't have done/felt that*), and release those thoughts. They aren't relevant right now. You're not passing judgment on the other person's experience; you're trying to *feel* it.

Reflect back to the other person what it felt like to try to understand that experience from their perspective. Do your best to talk about feelings and what you understood. For example, you might say, "I could really relate to that feeling because . . ." or, "I understand why you'd feel this way, because . . ."

Finally, think about how this felt different than the usual way you'd listen to or have a conversation with someone. Listening to understand someone else's feelings creates a deeper level of connection and shared humanity, which builds support for both the person who tells their story and the person who hears it.

If you feel you're "too" empathetic, or that getting in touch with other people's feelings affects you to an extreme degree, it can be helpful to practice empathy with boundaries. *Boundaries* is a buzzword, for sure—but for good reason. Younger generations are seeing the need to protect their personal space and energy rather than taking on more than they can handle or letting others affect them more than they want. By definition, boundaries are edges; they are where we end and other people begin. In therapy, we talk about personal boundaries as being the rules and limits we hold for ourselves in relationship to others. Maybe you know some people who have pretty firm boundaries—people who don't let others get too close, are very private, and are slow to "warm up." Maybe you also know people with very loose or nonexistent boundaries—people who let others "walk all over" them, overshare about themselves, or engage in gossip about others. These two ends of the spectrum are not ideal. On one hand, someone who has boundaries that are too rigid risks losing out on the support they need. On the other hand, someone who has boundaries that are too loose might lose themselves in favor of others' feelings or opinions. Ideally, our boundaries are more balanced and flexible; they might shift in different settings or with different people, depending on the expectations or need for protecting yourself or others. What you share and what you want to know and feel from others may be different at work than it is at home. It may also be different with acquaintances than it is with close friends or family members.

With empathy, boundaries are important so that you don't get lost in someone else's experience or feelings to the point that you don't recognize they belong to someone else. This could mean taking on someone else's feelings with such fervor that they become your own. This robs the other person of their ownership of those feelings, since you've co-opted or appropriated someone else's experience instead of sharing in it. It could also mean failing to recognize that a key piece of empathy is the *otherness* of the experience. The benefit to you is to feel connected to another person through shared emotions, not to feel your own emotions and associate them with someone else.

PRACTICE: *Holding Empathy with Boundaries*

When you feel especially affected by someone else's feelings or experience, use this visualization technique to help yourself hold those feelings while allowing for some distance.

1. Imagine a boundary around you. This boundary can look like whatever feels comforting to you: a low wall, a fence, a bubble, a window, and so on. Make it something that you can see over or through but is still a distinct border. On the other side of that boundary is the other person. They may be close to you or quite a distance away, but you can see them and feel their presence.

2. Visualize that this person's experiences, emotions, and thoughts all exist within their periphery and that yours are within yours. The experiences and feelings may flow over the boundary or through it as they're taken into your experience and become part of yours. But just as you have a boundary that allows certain things of yours to cross over, so does the other person. You are responsible for determining what crosses your boundary, when, and for how long.

3. Hold a thought or a feeling of the other person's for a time, but recognize that it is theirs. Then, release the thought or feeling back to them and hold what is yours. There is a fluidity to this sharing that happens for a time but doesn't become yours.

4. When you're deeply affected by something that another person shares, know that your response is your own but what was shared is not. The sharing may become part of your experience, but it's helpful to think about the sharing as separate from the experience that was shared.

5. To maintain this boundary when you're in a relationship with another person, tell them how their words or story affected you.

6. Speaking this out loud creates a border between what *they* shared and *your* response. This lets them know you're respecting that their experience was their own, yet it impacted you and how you feel. Saying so also creates a connection and a shared experience through empathy.

Gossip is a common misdirection of empathy or sympathy that ultimately decimates relationships and undermines support instead of strengthening it. Sharing something about someone else—regardless of whether your intentions are good or helpful—is another way of taking their experience on as your own. Gossip culture is prevalent in our world today, as we have more access to information about celebrities and other people than we ever have before. It's also prevalent in social media and mom groups, and it can often be enticing to dissect someone else's decisions and life in a way that we think makes us feel better about our own.

Gossip is often used to form connections. Think about when your mom or aunt might call you to tell you something "juicy" about another relative. It's meant to share in the emotional nature of someone else's situation. But talking about people behind their backs or in a malicious or judgmental way ultimately doesn't make us feel better about ourselves. It also doesn't create real, emotional closeness with the person we share the tea with. If anything, it creates and furthers an us-versus-them mentality that can make you feel more isolated and untrusting of others around you.

PRACTICE: *Defying Gossip Culture*

Think through how you want to respond to gossip as it plays out in your life. Maybe you have a family member, friend, or coworker who often looks to gossip with you. Or maybe you feel drawn to reading gossip about celebrities or others on social media.

Next, reflect on the feelings that come up when you're involved in gossip. Maybe there is some excitement or interest. Maybe there are other feelings as well: guilt, uneasiness, or fear or worry that someone might gossip about *you*. The uncomfortable feelings you feel about participating in gossip will tell you whether it sits well (or not) with you or whether the excitement you get from it is (or isn't) authentic or true to you and who you want to be.

Then, imagine how you could respond to gossip in a way that would be true to you. How would you want someone to respond if they were faced with gossipy information about you? Can you sense and practice a more nonjudgmental way of connecting with people that you'd like to gently or directly offer when gossip comes up? It can be as simple as walking away from the conversation or as direct as saying, "I don't like to engage in gossip. It doesn't feel good to me and it usually hurts people's feelings." Think about and practice what you'd like to say or do when gossip comes up around you.

SHARED HUMANITY AND MATERNITY

Being mothers connects us all to something bigger: a community of mothers that is more vast than most of us can even imagine. Thinking about your belonging to this bigger group and how many other mothers you're connected to just by virtue of being a mom can help when you feel lonely, isolated, or unacknowledged for your hard work. Keeping in mind our shared belonging in a collective of mothers is a way of bringing the power and strength of *all of us* when we need it.

Kristin Neff does encouraging research on the topic of self-compassion and notes that self-compassion has three main parts: mindfulness, in that we have to recognize feelings in ourselves such as pain or suffering; warm, caring response, in that we notice pain and act with care toward it rather than trying to stop it; and a sense of shared humanity, in that others have felt the way we feel and that our feelings connect us to everyone else and their struggles or pain.[6] We've already worked on those first two points so far in this book, and this section is about the third.

The connection you have to other mothers—those in your own generation, nearby or all over the world, as well as those in your family, your ancestors, and past generations of mothers—is powerful. We rarely stop to think how connected we all are by the experience of having a child, regardless of whether and how we gave birth to that child or whether we adopted, fostered, or acted as surrogate to them—or *however* we got here. We are a whole coalition of mothers. The importance of mothering is as old as time and as far-reaching as every animal species on earth.

This idea is both reassuring and humbling. None of us are alone in what we're going through. However unique you may feel in your mothering journey, hundreds—if not thousands—have gone through something similar to you. You are *not* alone. At the same time, you are one of millions and millions of mothers throughout time! The day-to-day struggles that might feel unbearable are just drops in the ocean of the experience and what it means to be a mother.

Being a part of something bigger is an innate human need. We all need to feel connected to others and to a greater good, a sense of shared experience in that others have been where we are and have come through the other side. There is evidence that we "encode," or feel the situation differently, when we experience it with someone else than when we go through it ourselves, especially when we're going through something difficult.[7,8] So your mindset about whether you're going through the hard times of motherhood alone (or not) is important to how you feel about it.

Maybe you have heard the word *sorority*, especially if you attended college or university. The definition of *sorority* is "sisterhood," which is what this institution is based on: connection through shared circumstance. In the same way, maternity—or motherhood—bonds us together with all of the mothers who have come before us and those who will come after. By whatever means you became a mother, it was enough. You're part of the maternity—or, if you prefer, the matriarchy—now. The two words are related, of course. Both come from *mater*, which is Latin for "mother." The word *matriarchy* also contains *arkhein*, which is Greek for "to rule." Whichever word feels most fulfilling, strengthening, and inclusive to you is your way of imagining the alliance of mothers you now belong to.

PRACTICE: *Immersing Yourself in Shared Maternity*

When you're struggling or feeling alone in your struggle, call to mind all of the mothers who are out there around the world. There are millions of us, engaged in our own struggles as well as in hard things that are similar to what you might be going through.

Next, think about the mothers who came before you, and the millions of mothers who will come after you. Reflect on this powerful, amazing group of mothers throughout time. Consider how this multitude of mothers is a force around and with you any time you need us. Feel the strength, wisdom, and love of all of these mothers wash over you and surround you.

Sharing the strength you find as a mother is important not just because it can help another new mom feel more confident and a little less lost, overwhelmed, or in survival mode. It can also spread a new message about motherhood— that it's a powerful and inspiring journey, rather than a self-sacrificing, lonely, anxiety-filled way of existing through your baby's first years.

Our society's views on motherhood are tangled up with the views on womanhood and the ideals of women to be small, quiet, weak, and selfless. Think about the disrespect these messages pay to our strongest and most valuable members—mothers, those who are charged with the continuation and care of the future of humanity! Why on earth should we be expected to be small and quiet? Why should we be meek and selfless? Let's instead claim our strength, our power, our SELVES! Let's take pride in who we are instead of trying to fit ourselves into old standards that are stale, judgmental, and designed to make us feel bad about ourselves. We get to set a new standard of women and mothers by accepting ourselves—all of us, for our strengths *and* our flaws—as perfect just the way we are.

PRACTICE: *Changing Your View of Motherhood*

Practice associating motherhood (or whatever word you prefer for your experience of parenthood) with strength. When you think about the mothers in your life (including yourself), visualize symbols of power, might, ability, skill, energy, and intensity. Do this in different settings or states of mind, no matter if you feel strong yourself or if you're feeling overwhelmed or defeated.

When this connection between motherhood and strength becomes more familiar or comfortable to you, consider how you can share about your experience of motherhood in a way that empowers other mothers. Maybe you can post about your child or your day on social media, or send an encouraging message to another mom in your life. Find ways to incorporate this powerful vision of motherhood into the way you believe in, portray, or present yourself as a mother. Recognize the power in how creating this new message about motherhood can ripple out and influence others.

WATCHING YOUR LANGUAGE

What you say matters.

The language we use matters. Think about how you feel if someone gets your name wrong or refers to your baby as *it* instead of a human pronoun. If we're conscious of the words we use by practicing nonjudgmental language (to ourselves as well as to others), we can show that it's important to us to understand another person's experience and support it rather than closing ourselves off and appearing aloof or critical. People aren't likely to look to you for support if they think you're judgmental or you don't understand where they're coming from or what they're going through.

When it comes to helping others, we're best served by reserving our judgments and opening ourselves to that person's perspective and situation. We want to use nonjudgmental language so that we don't shut down someone else based on our own judgments or opinions. More importantly, the words you use reflect your attitudes and might trigger shame for other moms. If you speak harshly about using formula instead of breastfeeding, a mom who needed to use formula because she struggled with breastfeeding might interpret your words as shaming and get so lost in her own feelings about it that she can't open up to you about her struggles.

Our words might hit someone in unintentional ways, especially if we don't know their history. A mom who has had a miscarriage might prickle at your complaining about your baby being up all night. Another mother who works multiple jobs and saves every penny to feed her family might shut down when you offer advice that she "has to" buy the newest baby gadget or service. Other moms might fall into feelings of shame because they wish they could have what you have and feel like it's somehow their fault that they don't. You don't want to be a source of unintended shame for new moms. So it's up to you to think about how your words reflect your attitudes and may trigger shame for others. Often this means identifying what judgments are bubbling up and seeing whether you can speak out of openness and acceptance instead of that judgmental voice.

PRACTICE: *Using Nonjudgmental Language*

Watch the words you're drawn to using in conversation. How often do you rely on critical or subjective words such as *good, bad, right*, or *wrong* (or other versions of these words)? These words focus on expressing your opinions about what the other person is saying rather than listening and being open to their experience.

Listen fully, so you can understand what the other person is saying. Reflect what makes sense to you back to them, and ask curious questions to learn about what feels unclear. The goal is to see the other person's perspective rather than sharing your own.

Respond with observations, acceptance, and encouragement. Advice and opinions are meant to end the conversation, not to continue it. Unless someone has specifically asked for advice, giving it only serves to shut the other person down. Letting the other person know what you observe when they're talking (e.g., "You were upset by what your friend said," "You get tearful when you talk about that situation") shows them that you're paying attention rather than figuring out what to say next. Using words that convey acceptance (e.g., "It's okay," "That makes sense," "I hear you") makes the other person feel heard and valued, and they may be likely to share more with you.

Substitute curiosity. The antidote to falling into judgment (about ourselves or others) is curiosity. When you feel like it's hard to reserve judgment, see if you can reframe the judgment (e.g., "You must feel . . . ," "Don't feel that way") into a curious question, such as "What does it feel like?" or "Why do you think you feel that way?" Asking a question instead of stating an opinion opens the conversation and allows for more understanding, which will lead to less judgment.

Think about the kinds of support you needed in your journey as a new mom. Back in chapter 3 we talked about these different types of support. (Go back to page 60 if you want to refresh your memory.) Which of these was hardest for you to find? How can you offer that kind of support for another new mom? She may need it as much as you did.

Keep in mind, though, that if you're offering someone a particular kind of support because you feel strongly that they need it, you may be basing your support on a judgment—and any kind of advice or care that's offered out of judgment isn't likely to be well received. If, for instance, you see that a baby's ears are pierced and you respond with anger because you disagree with this parenting choice, you're judging that mother by believing she has done something to harm her child. A less judgmental way of looking at the situation would be to recognize that you know very little about this woman's life or culture. From that lens, think about how you can let your opinion go unstated or get to know this mom better. That way, you can challenge your instinct to be critical with your ability to be open and curious. In order to be truly supportive of other moms, we have to let our own agenda go and be there for others in the ways they need us to be.

An important part of offering support is knowing that someone may not want a particular kind of support from you. Just because we want to help someone else doesn't mean they want to be helped in a certain way (or at all). Below are some ways you can offer or build your capacity to support without forcing it on someone who doesn't need it.

PRACTICE: *Offering Support without Judgment*

Guidance: If you're drawn to offering advice or information about your experience to another mom, reflect on your intentions for sharing this. If you're hoping to show how much you know about the situation or to prove a point, then don't share. This isn't guidance or support but rather a way to stoke your own ego. But if you determine that you want to share something in hopes that it will help the other person, ask them questions such as, "Can I share something about my experience?" or "Can I give you some advice?" to see if they're open to your guidance rather than jumping in with it. Share your experience or information you know, and avoid saying what you think the other mom should do. Remember that the word "should" conveys judgment or that there is a right or wrong way to handle the situation, which there isn't.

Alliance: If you're interested in allying with or offering assistance to a mom, think about why you want to do this. What draws you to this other person? It's likely that you see them in need of something that you possess, or that you feel an affinity for them for some reason. Act out of these motives, and ensure your intentions are clear. Being transparent and centered in your feelings allows you to approach the alliance from an empathetic mindset, which also requires you to ask whether the other person wants your help or alliance. And if they don't, that's okay. As long as you've been honest about your intentions, it's no affront to you if they don't want or need what you're offering.

Reassurance: If you feel an urge to recognize or reassure another mom, then do it! It's hard to get enough reassurance or recognition. But it's also important to recognize that people have different feelings about how they want to be recognized or reassured. Saying something privately initially will give them an opportunity to let you know whether and how they're comfortable receiving this kind of support. Let go of expectations or qualifiers such as, "You're doing a great job, but . . ." or "I hope you will . . ." These kinds of statements redirect your praise or reassurance into something more focused on you than them. Keep the focus on what you want the other mom to feel good about.

Attachment: If you want to develop emotional closeness with another mom, remember that it's all about sharing feelings. This means you need to be prepared to share your feelings—and you also need to be prepared to hear, attend to, and draw out someone else's feelings. If you're the one who wants the closeness, you have to go first. Start with something easy, such as letting the other mom know something about new motherhood that has been hard for you. Ask them how it has been for them, and focus on what they say using those empathy skills discussed earlier in this chapter. Reflect the other person's words back to them to show you understand or relate to what they said.

Social Integration: If you're relating to another mom because of shared interests or activities, it can be helpful to deepen this connection so that you can offer other kinds of support if needed. Connecting through shared interest can often lead to connection in other areas. The above practice for attachment is one way of doing this. Remember that it's equally important to share your experience and allow for differences. Just because you and another mom both enjoy something, doesn't mean the shared interest fills the same need for the other mom as it does for you, or that the other mom has the same reasons as you for engaging in it. Getting to know these differences can also enrich your experience of the activity.

Nurturance: Supporting other people's well-being is probably the deepest and hardest level of support. It's very much about letting go of our own judgments about how anyone *should* be and just loving what *is*. Nurturing someone very often means nurturing ourselves, too, so that we're capable of setting judgmental or biased thinking aside and not feeling the need to have "conditions" on our love and care. If you want to support other moms' well-being, start internally and see how you best receive care and love. Then see how it feels to shine that light outward to another mom without expectation of reciprocation or recognition.

You may have noticed a theme in the above practice: make sure the support is about the other person, not you. This is what support truly is—providing something to someone else. Yes, you can certainly hope that the other person will reciprocate when and how you need it. But offering support to someone else is best done without expectation of reciprocation. That way, it becomes a connection instead of a transaction. Transactions are one-sided, since they're about one person having power or status above the other. Think of it as if you're at a bank to take out money, and the bank has all the authority because they can accept or deny your request no matter what your reason for needing that money.

What we're looking for when we want to support another new mom or receive the same support isn't a transaction. It's a human connection. To achieve that kind of connection, we have to be willing to approach the relationship with vulnerability. We need to bring our deep care and consideration of the other person's humanity and perspective. If we're not willing to do that, we might not be in the right mindset to make or maintain those connections. In that case, it's better to wait until we feel more centered and able to approach with vulnerability and care; or else we might stumble through or muck it up. It's okay if your attempts at connection don't go as planned. At least you're trying!

If you have an interaction with an existing friend or support person or a potential new one that doesn't go well, the next best thing you can do is be open to repairing things. We're going to make mistakes, miscommunicate, or react in ways we wish we wouldn't. What matters is what we do afterward. We can leave the relationship alone or we can do our best to repair it. These "relationship ruptures" can become like wounds that need to be treated in order to get better. Leaving the relationship alone might make it feel less awkward or painful for the moment, but it also leaves it raw and open rather than allowing it to heal over. Gottman Institute found that attempting repair is key to successful relationships.[9] Repair often means allowing yourself to cool down emotionally before revisiting the conversation from a different lens.

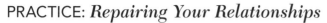

PRACTICE: *Repairing Your Relationships*

If an interaction with your partner, a friend, or an acquaintance didn't go as planned, think about how you might attempt to repair it.

1. **Consider whether your feelings were hurt or whether fear, anger, or worry got in the way of understanding.** The first step is identifying how the interaction affected you emotionally and giving yourself some validation that there is likely a reason for whatever you are feeling.

2. **See what you can offer to yourself to soothe your feelings.** It might be time, a day to "sleep on it," or time away and on your own for self-care. Care for your feelings so that you can see the interaction from a calmer, more peaceful place.

3. **Identify if you feel sorry about some part of the interaction.** Did you say something in a way you didn't mean? Did you offend the other person? No matter what, this is the lead-in to your attempt at repairing the relationship. So think about how you can apologize in an honest and authentic way for your part of whatever went awry in the conversation.

4. **Think about what you want for your relationship after the repair (if repair can be made).** What do you hope for with this relationship or future interactions? Do you hope that the two of you can be closer? That you can both be honest about how you feel?

Ask the other person to let you know when they're ready to talk. Begin with any apology you'd like to make authentically, as well as what you hope for if the relationship can be repaired. Then open up and listen to the other person's perspective, whatever it may be.

Remember to let go of a specific outcome. The relationship might not be repairable in the way you want it to be. Your attempt at repair is all that you can do; the other person also gets to have a say in how this turns out. So be as honest and open as you can be, then allow yourself to soften or welcome their thoughts, feelings, and feedback.

BRAVE NEW MOMS

There are all kinds of brave new moms out there. There are single moms by choice, older moms, younger moms, working moms, stay-at-home moms, Instagram moms, adoptive moms, and moms who have lost their babies. There are mamas, mums, single moms, married moms, polyamorous moms, separated or divorced moms, and widowed moms. There are lesbian and bisexual moms, moms who are part of a same-sex or polyamorous relationship, nonbinary and transgender parents or birthing people who might not identify as moms but carry all the same struggles and so many more. There are Black moms who enter motherhood through dangerously racist systems of care and are three to four times more likely to die on their journey to joining our community.[10]

My hope is that we are brave and strong enough to love, accept, and support them all.

During the 2020 COVID-19 pandemic (which was happening as I was writing this book), we saw what happens when a mother's mental health is ignored by society and then pushed to its limits. New moms became more isolated, strained, fearful, unsupported, and distressed than ever before.[11] And in one recent study, most new moms reported feeling anxious during the pandemic, and almost half reported feeling lonely.[12] Self-care and support were (and possibly still are) the two most helpful practices for those who are struggling. So we need to take good care of ourselves and encourage other new moms to do the same. We also need to find ways to reach out and support each other during unprecedented times.

If you've felt even a budge in your self-confidence or enjoyment as a new mom while reading this book, you know how monumental it is to *feel better* about how you're doing. Through this brave new lens you know that happiness isn't limited. There is enough for all of us. If we feel good about how *we're* doing, we'll want that for every new mom or parent who is living in survival mode. We want them all to feel just a little better, a little braver, and a little more like they know what they're doing—and that it's enough.

It might be hard to think about supporting and loving all moms out there. You might not feel strong or secure enough in yourself to help anyone else. You may feel fearful about what it would mean to unlearn some of the judgments you've held your whole life and have never known yourself without. In fact, it can feel incredibly freeing to let go of those worries. Let's practice what it would feel like to radiate strength and support to those around you.

PRACTICE: *Meditating on Loving-Kindness toward All Mothers*

This is a wonderful meditation to practice when you feel conflicted or are craving a sense of calm, caring, or connectedness.

Start with yourself. Think or say these words out loud, and allow them to sink in deeply:

May I be peaceful and happy.
May I be healthy and strong.
May I be filled with loving kindness.
May I be free.

Next, think about a loved one. Again, think or say these words out loud, and allow them to surround your loved one:

May they be peaceful and happy.
May they be healthy and strong.
May they be filled with loving kindness.
May they be free.

Then, think of someone you have trouble with. Allow yourself to reflect on these words toward that person:

May they be peaceful and happy.
May they be healthy and strong.
May they be filled with loving kindness.
May they be free.

Finally, think about all mothers everywhere. Bring them all to your mind, and send out these wishes to them:

May they be peaceful and happy.
May they be healthy and strong.
May they be filled with loving kindness.
May they be free.

*Adapted from Sharon Salzberg's *guided loving-kindness meditation* at mindful.org.[13]

What a beautiful thought. We can all be peaceful, strong, kind, and at ease—and it doesn't cost us anything to wish the same for everyone else. We're all going to go through hard things in motherhood and in our lives; and we can either brace ourselves and survive through them, or we can "brave" ourselves because of them and see them as evidence of our strength and resilience.

Think back to the help and support that felt the best to you when you were a brand-new mom, as well as what you would have liked to receive, but didn't. These are the things that other new moms need from us! One concrete thing you can do is pass on this book (if you found it helpful) to another new mom you know. If you've written all over and dog-eared the pages, then buy another copy for her at this link: www.bravenewmom.org/book with a discount for brave new moms (code: iambrave).

Here are other ways you can offer support to new moms:

PRACTICE: *Offering Support to Other New Moms*

If you know a new mom, offer her some direct support in any of the following ways:

1. Bring her food! Ask her if there is anything she would really love to have, or surprise her with something you think she might like.

2. Give her a gift card or certificate she can use to shop online or go to the store in person.

3. Ask if she would like to chat, either in person or over the phone. Let her know you're there to listen whenever she is having a hard time. And if she takes you up on this, refer to the earlier practices *Using Nonjudgmental Language* and *Offering Support without Judgment.*

4. Offer to visit and bring her anything she might need, or to be with her baby while she takes a nap or does some self-care. Remind her that you won't judge her house, appearance, cleanliness, or parenting (and then don't!).

5. Let her know that you're willing to be there any time (or set some boundaries, if you need to) for advice, reassurance, venting, recognition, or validation. Tell her you understand that she needs these things and that you're willing to be there for her when she needs you.

6. Offer to engage in self-care or shared interests together if/when she is ready. Let her know you understand the feelings of mom guilt and being in survival mode. That way, when she needs a reprieve, you'll be there to help get her out and excited to take care of herself away from her baby.

owning your strength

If you don't know any new moms but want to offer support to moms more broadly, here are a few things you can do:

1. Donate to mom-centered or mom-owned companies that focus on helping other parents. Some of the big ones are Together Rising, Baby2Baby, Every Mother Counts, Parents as Teachers, Help a Mother Out, Global Fund for Women, and Carry the Future. You'll also find there are many in your local community that support families and mothers in different ways.

2. Be a positive force for mothers on social media. If you belong to any mom groups or generally post about motherhood on your social pages, look for ways to make your voice a positive, uplifting, and nonjudgmental, supportive one for other mothers out there who might be prone to feeling bad about themselves or using social media to compare themselves to others. Challenge yourself to join some mom groups that you're not already part of or to post purposefully uplifting comments on any negative or judgmental posts you see to offer a different way of supporting other mothers.

3. Get involved at the legislative level. New moms rarely have the time or energy to put toward advocacy, even in matters that affect them directly. So if *you* have time and energy, look at all of the bills focused on motherhood issues in your area and get in contact by writing letters and calling your local representatives. Search "legislative bills about mothers," or visit the Moms Rising website at www.momsrising.org for some of the important topics in your region.

What other things were helpful to you when you were a new mom? Write them below:

What other things would have been helpful when you were a new mom but weren't available? Write them below:

CHAPTER 7 CHECKLIST

Here are the practices you learned in this chapter:

1. Cultivating Empathy
2. Holding Empathy with Boundaries
3. Defying Gossip Culture
4. Immersing Yourself in Shared Maternity
5. Changing Your View of Motherhood
6. Using Nonjudgmental Language
7. Offering Support without Judgment
8. Repairing Your Relationships
9. Meditating on Loving-Kindness toward All Mothers
10. Offering Support to Other New Moms

Pick two favorites from the list above. Write them on a piece of paper and tape it to your bathroom mirror. Make the practices that were useful to you a part of your daily routine, and consider marking the ones that were harder to connect with so you can explore them further or try them again later. Practice doesn't make perfect, but it helps to make it a habit and deepen the positive effects the more you try these exercises.

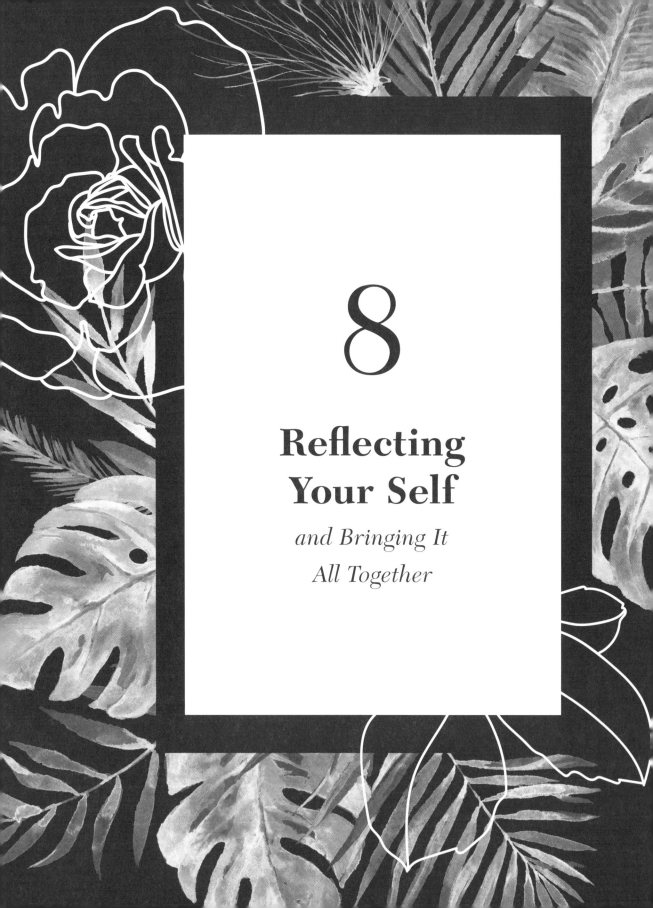

8

Reflecting Your Self

*and Bringing It
All Together*

WE'VE SPENT OUR TIME TOGETHER
practicing new ways of experiencing new motherhood through self-care, honoring your feelings and experiences, building social support, allowing for difficulty, affirming your strength, and connecting with yourself and others in meaningful ways. So as this book comes to a close, it's a good idea to reflect on the progress you've made through deliberate practice. Also, consider integrating what worked here into your path through motherhood.

I hope that you've gained a little in nurturing a feeling of openness and acceptance toward yourself and others. Examining where you have judgments (and why) and where you can relax or let go of these judgments allows you to observe and feel the hard things you go through without struggling against them, denying them, or defining yourself by them. Cultivating this feeling of openness and acceptance for yourself helps you see the world in a more open and accepting light. This creates a cycle of improved well-being and perspective on how you and everyone else around you are doing. Acceptance of yourself, your strengths, your flaws, and everything in between is key to feeling like you've got this. Now that you know we all go through it, you can stop judging yourself so harshly.

You probably feel like we've done a lot of *breathing*. It's true—we have. Conscious, focused breathing is the best tool we have to bring ourselves out of fight-or-flight survival mode and into a calmer way of being in the moment. You have your breath with you wherever you go, whether your baby is screaming in the grocery store or you're at home and feeling anxious or lonely. If you found useful ways to connect to your breath, you now have a powerful instrument in your arsenal to battle through stressors or to just get through the day. While you breathe all the time, making a practice of doing it consciously, calmly, and lovingly is a gift you can give yourself whenever you need it.

We also talked a lot about self-care. I hope that you take away from this book a feeling that you're worthy of and in need of as much care as you give to others. Self-care is as important as breathing. It's the first step in caring for your baby, your family, and anyone else in the world. It starts with you—and you deserve your own attention every day! Being conscious and intentional about taking good care of yourself is a brave and powerful act in motherhood. Being a mother is such a generous and mighty role that you carry, and it's not the only one. Remember that *you* get to be the priority sometimes, and that you're more than any one thing that you do, including being a mom. Self-care is taking care of *all* of the parts of you that make you who you are.

The experience of new motherhood is a lot of things, so it's going to be difficult sometimes. I hope that you've felt evidence of our collective motherhood around this—that all moms go through hard things, and that we can both accept and work to change our responses to them if we want to. You are capable of going through hard things, surviving, persisting, and emerging stronger and more resilient because of them. Keeping track of that strength and resilience through the hard things, as well as accepting them for what they are instead of denying or resisting them, helps us bear them and bear witness to them as things that shape us but don't break us.

We also spent a lot of time talking about connecting to yourself and others. Even the most introverted or solitary among us are not islands. We need to feel connected to each other so that we know we're not alone in our struggles. In some ways, connecting to ourselves and to others are two sides of the same coin. The same skills and practices that put you more in touch with yourself through brambles of judgments and beliefs will also help you reach out to others who might otherwise be obscured by those same brambles. The openness we cultivate toward ourselves makes it easier to be open and authentic with other people. Recognizing that you need support and connection also makes you see how powerful small acts of connection can be for one another.

Finally, we talked about keeping our eyes on the bigger picture—or at least reminding ourselves that there *is* a bigger picture—to make meaning out of the hard things we face. Being a mom is hard. It's also amazing, when you think about it. We're helping a little being survive. More than that, we're helping them grow, learn, be, and live in the world in ways that only we can. We are their *everything*, from before they even know it to the times when no one else might see it—but *we are*. Seeing the beauty, the amazing, the immense responsibility, and the immense miracle of it makes the million hard things just drops in the bucket of what we're actually doing here.

Now that you've identified some areas where you need the most help staying present, hopeful, and self-compassionate, it's time to put together a plan for yourself. These challenges will come up not only during this new mom phase but also afterward, and knowing what you know doesn't inoculate you from tough things happening to you. Life (and children) will throw hard things at you, and it's up to you to keep doing your best, handling things with the strength you've found in yourself and allowing them to happen but not to knock you down.

PRACTICE: *Plan for Thoughts and Feelings*

Identify which of the following strategies from chapter 2 are most helpful when you're dealing with unhelpful thoughts or difficult emotions, and make a plan for when to use them:

- Identifying Your Feelings (page 39)
- Engaging Mindfully with Your Partner (page 40)
- Separating Yourself from Guilt (page 41)
- Identifying Your Sensations and Feelings (page 42)
- Observing Your Feelings Nonjudgmentally (page 45)

- Working Through Feelings of Loss (page 48)
- Calming Yourself with Deep Breathing (page 50)
- Slowing Down Your Reaction (page 52)
- Savoring Positive Feelings (page 53)
- Getting Out of Your Head (page 54)

How will you know you need to use these strategies?

How can you use them proactively (i.e., before you need them)?

PRACTICE: *Plan for Self-Care*

Identify which of the self-care activities in the Building In Self-Care practice (see chapter 1, page 28) are most helpful to you, and make a plan for when to use them below.

List self-care activities you have identified that work for you.

How often do you plan to do self-care?

What are the barriers you experience to practicing self-care?

How can you overcome these barriers? How can you ensure you'll practice self-care when you need it?

PRACTICE: *Plan for Stressful Times*

List your strengths below. Revisit the Focusing on Your Strengths practice in chapter 4, page 83, if you need help.

Identify your early warning signs of stress, and create a coping plan for each one below.

Signs that I'm Stressed	What I Can Do When This Happens
Physical Sensations:	
Feelings/Emotions:	
Behaviors/Actions:	
Negative Thoughts:	

What things can you do regularly to *prevent* getting overly stressed?

Look back at your strengths and see whether any of them can give you more ideas for supporting yourself when you're dealing with hard things.

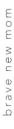

brave new mom

PRACTICE: *Plan for Connection*

Identify three people you can reach out to when you need help.

Identify the types of support you need and who you can reach out to for each one.

If there are any gaps in support (i.e., you don't have a person in your life who can provide a specific kind of support), write about how you can broaden your circle to get that kind of support.

Review the *Reflecting on Your Supports* and *Building Up Your Support System* activities on pages 60 and 62, respectively.

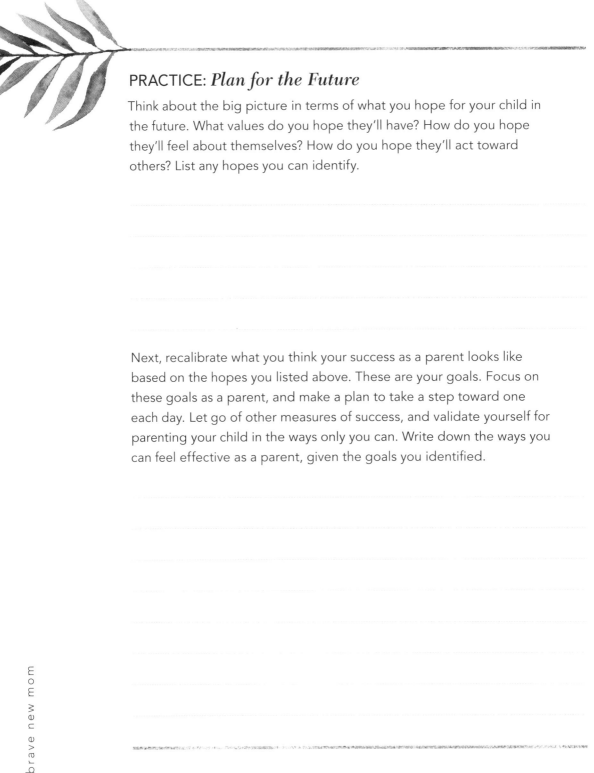

PRACTICE: *Plan for the Future*

Think about the big picture in terms of what you hope for your child in the future. What values do you hope they'll have? How do you hope they'll feel about themselves? How do you hope they'll act toward others? List any hopes you can identify.

Next, recalibrate what you think your success as a parent looks like based on the hopes you listed above. These are your goals. Focus on these goals as a parent, and make a plan to take a step toward one each day. Let go of other measures of success, and validate yourself for parenting your child in the ways only you can. Write down the ways you can feel effective as a parent, given the goals you identified.

CHAPTER 8 CHECKLIST

Here are the practices you learned in this chapter:

1. Plan for Thoughts and Feelings
2. Plan for Self-Care
3. Plan for Stressful Times
4. Plan for Connection
5. Plan for the Future

As you develop each plan, consider what you struggle with most as well as which practices help you come back to yourself and enjoy this period in your life. List those practices, then use them as part of your daily routine. Also, consider marking the exercises that were harder for you to connect with so you can explore them further or try them again later. Practice doesn't make perfect, but it helps to make it a habit and deepen the positive effects the more you try these exercises.

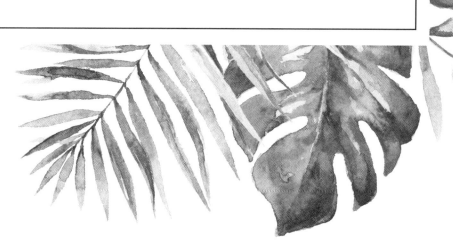

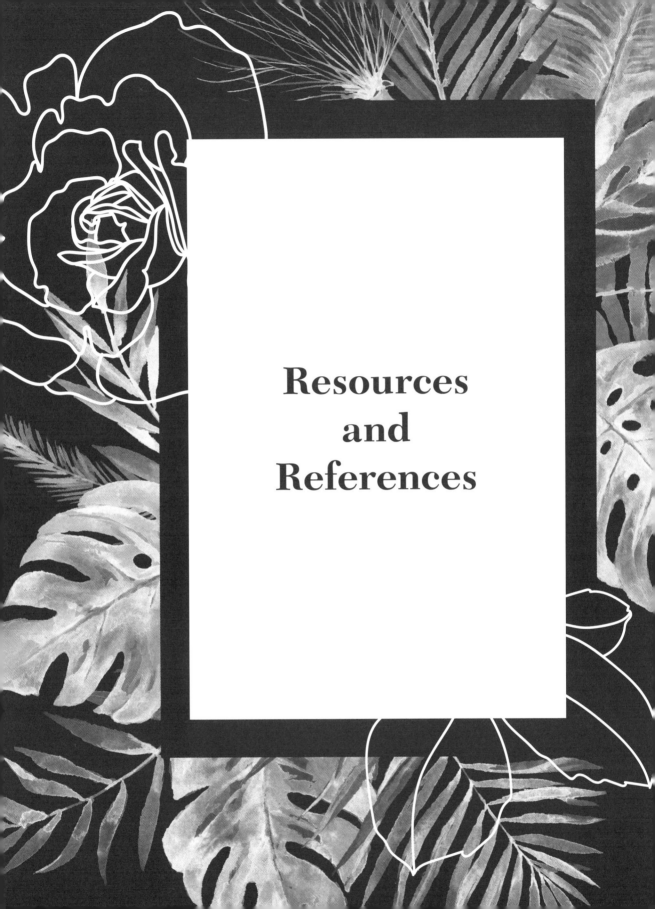

Resources
and
References

RESOURCES

POSTPARTUM SUPPORT INTERNATIONAL

Remember that if you have *any* thoughts about harming yourself or your baby, please reach out for help. Call PSI's helpline at 1-800-944-4773, or text them at that same number (for English-speaking users) or 971-420-0294 (for Spanish-speaking users). You can also visit PSI at www.postpartum.net to look up local resources in the United States and internationally as well as online support groups for perinatal (pregnant and postpartum) moods, pregnancy moods, NICU parents, pregnancy and infant loss, military moms, Black moms, and more.

BRAVENEWMOM.ORG

A community of moms who have been immersed in this book and who are committed to supporting each other is growing at www.bravenewmom.org.

NATIONAL SUICIDE PREVENTION LIFELINE

1-800-273-TALK (8255) or TTY: 1-800-799-4TTY (4889)

CRISIS TEXT LINE

Text "HELLO" to 741741

OTHER BOOKS TO CHECK OUT

Good Moms Have Scary Thoughts, by Karen Kleiman

This Isn't What I Expected: Overcoming Postpartum Depression, by Karen Kleiman and Valerie Davis Raskin

The Pregnancy & Postpartum Anxiety Workbook, by Pamela S. Wiegartz and Kevin L. Gyoerkoe

The Bottom Line for Baby, by Tina Payne Bryson

REFERENCES

CHAPTER 1—RECLAIMING YOUR POWER: FROM "WHAT HAVE I DONE?" TO "I HAVE DONE SOMETHING AMAZING"

1. Priya Soma-Pillay, Catherine Nelson-Piercy, Heli Tolppanen, and Alexandre Mebazaa, "Physiological changes in pregnancy," *Cardiovascular Journal of Africa* 27, no. 2 (March/April 2016): 89, https://doi.org/10.5830/CVJA-2016-021.

2. Gaurav Chauhan, "Physiology, Postpartum Changes," *StatPearls*, March 15, 2020, https://www.statpearls.com/articlelibrary/viewarticle/27550/.

3. Emma L. Hodgkinson, Debbie M. Smith, and Anja Wittkowski, "Women's experiences of their pregnancy and postpartum body image: a systematic review and meta-synthesis," *BMC Pregnancy and Childbirth* 14, 330 (2014), https://doi.org/10.1186/1471-2393-14-330.

4. "The First 42 Days," Aeroflow Breastpumps, accessed March 17, 2020, https://aeroflowbreastpumps.com/first-forty-two-days.

5. Teri Pearlstein, Margaret Howard, Amy Salisbury, and Caron Zlotnick, "Postpartum depression," *American Journal of Obstetrics and Gynecology* 200, no. 4 (April 1, 2009): 357, https://doi.org/10.1016/j.ajog.2008.11.033.

6. Pearlstein et al., "Postpartum depression," 357–364.

7. Cari Nierenberg, "Mood Swings & Mommy Brain: The Emotional Challenges of Pregnancy," *Live Science* (blog), December 22, 2017, https://www.livescience.com/51043-pregnancy-emotions.html.

8. "Depression Among Women," Centers for Disease Control and Prevention, March 19, 2020, https://www.cdc.gov/reproductivehealth/depression/index.htm.

9. Birdie Gunyon Meyer, "Perinatal Mood Disorders: Overview," Postpartum Support International, accessed December 5, 2019, https://www.postpartum.net/professionals/trainings-events/.

10. Susan Dowd Stone and Alexis E. Menken, *Perinatal and Postpartum Mood Disorders: Perspectives and Treatment Guide for the Health Care Practitioner* (New York: Springer Publishing Company, 2008), 66.

11. Christina Prinds, Niels Christian Hvidt, Ole Mogensen, and Niels Buus, "Making existential meaning in transition to motherhood— A scoping review," *Midwifery* 30, no. 6 (June 2014): 733, https://doi.org/10.1016/j.midw.2013.06.021.

12. Charlotte Elvander, Sven Cnattingius, and Kristen H. Kjerulff, "Birth experience in women with low, intermediate or high levels of fear: Findings from the First Baby Study," *Birth* 40, no. 4 (December 2013): 289, https://doi.org/10.1111/birt.12065.

13. Bessel van der Kolk, *The Body Keeps the Score: Brain, Mind, and Body in the Healing of Trauma* (New York: Penguin Books, 2015), 54.

14. Centers for Disease Control and Prevention National Vital Statistics Report, "Mean Age of Mother, 1970–2000," vol. 51, no. 1 (December 11, 2002): 10, https://www.cdc.gov/nchs/data/nvsr/nvsr51/nvsr51_01.pdf.

15. University of Essex, Institute for Social and Economic Research, *Understanding Society: Waves 1–9, 2009–2018 and Harmonised BHPS: Waves 1–18, 1991–2009*, 12th ed. (UK Data Service. SN: 6614), http://doi.org/10.5255/UKDA-SN-6614-13.

16. Gijs Beets, Joop Schippers, and Egbert R. te Velde, *The Future of Motherhood in Western Societies: Late Fertility and Its Consequences* (New York: Springer, 2011), 2.

17. Susanna Graham, "Chapter 7. Choosing single motherhood? Single women negotiating the nuclear family ideal," in *Families: Beyond the Nuclear Ideal*, ed. Daniela Cutas and Sarah Chan (London: Bloomsbury Academic, 2012): 97, http://dx.doi.org/10.5040/9781780930114.ch-007.

18. University of Essex, Institute for Social and Economic Research, *Understanding Society: Waves 1–9, 2009–2018 and Harmonised BHPS: Waves 1–18, 1991–2009*, 12th ed.

19. Lorraine Tulman, Jacqueline Fawcett, Laura Groblewski, and Lisa Silverman, "Changes in functional status after childbirth," *Nursing Research* 39, no. 2 (March/April 1990): 70–75, https://journals.lww.com/nursingresearchonline/Abstract/1990/03000/Changes_in_Functional_Status_After_Childbirth.2.aspx.

20. Jennifer L. Barkin and Katherine L. Wisner, "The role of maternal self-care in new motherhood," *Midwifery* 29 (2013): 1051, https://doi.org/10.1016/j.midw.2012.10.001.

21. Younglee Kim and Vivien Dee, "Self-Care for Health in Rural Hispanic Women at Risk for Postpartum Depression," *Maternal and Child Health Journal* 21, no. 1 (January 2017), 78, https://doi-org.ezp3.lib.umn.edu/10.1007/s10995-016-2096-8.

22. Jennifer L. Barkin, Katherine L. Wisner, Joyce T. Bromberger, Scott R. Beach, and Stephen R. Wisniewski, "Assessment of functioning in new mothers," Journal of Women's Health 19, no. 8 (2010), 1494, DOI: 10.1089=jwh.2009.1864.

23. Barkin & Wisner, "The role of maternal self-care in new motherhood."

24. Chimamanda Ngozi Adichie, *Dear Ijeawele, or A Feminist Manifesto in Fifteen Suggestions* (New York: Anchor Books, 2017), 7.

25. Barkin et al., "Assessment of functioning in new mothers."

26. Rob Jordan, "Stanford researchers find mental health prescription: Nature," *Stanford News*, June 30, 2015, https://news.stanford.edu/2015/06/30/hiking-mental-health-063015/.

27. Holli-Anne Passmore, and Mark Holder, "Noticing nature: Individual and social benefits of a two-week intervention," *The Journal of Positive Psychology* 12, no. 6 (July 2016): 537, https://doi.org/10.1080/17439760.2016.1221126.

28. Association for Psychological Science, "Grin and bear it: Smiling facilitates stress recovery," *ScienceDaily*, July 30, 2012, www.sciencedaily.com/releases/2012/07/120730150113.htm.

29. Tulman et al., "Changes in functional status after childbirth," 70.

CHAPTER 2—RECOVERING YOUR SPIRIT: FROM "IS WHAT I'M FEELING OKAY?" TO "MY FEELINGS MATTER"

1. Nierenberg, "Mood Swings & Mommy Brain: The Emotional Challenges of Pregnancy."

2. Meyer, "Perinatal Mood Disorders: Overview."

3. "Baby Blues," American Pregnancy Association, last modified January 25, 2019, https://americanpregnancy.org/healthy-pregnancy/first-year-of-life/baby-blues-71032.

4. Karen Kleiman and Valerie Davis Raskin, *This Isn't What I Expected: Overcoming Postpartum Depression* (Boston: Da Capo Lifelong Books, 2013), 236.

5. April Eldemire, "Research Shows a Couple's Friendship is Key to Reducing Postpartum Depression," *The Gottman Institute* (blog), February 8, 2017, https://www.gottman.com/blog/research-shows-couples-friendship-key-reducing-postpartum-depression/.

6. Ira Kantrowitz-Gordon, "Factor structure and external validity of the five facet mindfulness questionnaire in pregnancy," *Mindfulness* 9 (2018), 247.

7. Judy Slome Cohain, Rina E. Buxbaum, and David Mankuta, "Spontaneous first trimester miscarriage rates per woman among parous women with 1 or more pregnancies of 24 weeks or more," *BMC Pregnancy Childbirth* 17, 437 (2017), https://doi.org/10.1186/s12884-017-1620-1.

8. Paul E. Jose, Bee T. Lim, and Fred B. Bryant, "Does savoring increase happiness? A daily diary study," *The Journal of Positive Psychology*, 7, 3 (2012), 177, DOI: 10.1080/17439760.2012.671345.

9. Fred B. Bryant, and Joseph Veroff, *Savoring: A new model of positive experience.* (Mahwah, NJ: Lawrence Erlbaum Associates, 2007), 2.

10. Shaila Misri, Pratibha Reebye, Lisa Milis, and Sharita Shah, "The impact of treatment intervention on parenting stress in postpartum depressed mothers: A prospective study," *American Journal of Orthopsychiatry* 76, no. 1 (2006): 118, https://doi.org/10.1037/0002-9432.76.1.115.

CHAPTER 3—EMBRACING YOUR COMMUNITY: FROM "I FEEL ALONE IN THIS" TO "I AM WORTHY OF LOVE AND SUPPORT"

1. Pamela S. Wiegartz and Kevin L. Gyoerkoe, *The Pregnancy and Postpartum Anxiety Workbook: Practical Skills to Help You Overcome Anxiety, Worry, Panic Attacks, Obsessions, and Compulsions* (Oakland, California: New Harbinger Publications, 2009), 8.

2. Alexandra B. Balaji, Angelika H. Claussen, D. Camille Smith, Susanna N. Visser, Melody Johnson Morales, and Ruth Perou, "Social Support Networks and Maternal Mental Health and Well-Being," *Journal of Women's Health* 16, no. 10 (December 7, 2007): 1388, https://doi.org/10.1089/jwh.2007.CDC10.

3. Cindy-Lee Dennis and Lori Ross, "Women's perceptions of partner support and conflict in the development of postpartum depressive symptoms," *Journal of Advanced Nursing* 56, no. 6 (December 2006): 594, https://doi.org/10.1111/j.1365-2648.2006.04059.x.

4. R.H. Glazier, F.J. Elgar, V. Goel, and S. Holzapfel, "Stress, social support, and emotional distress in a community sample of pregnant women," *Journal of Psychosomatic Obstetrics & Gynecology* 25, 3–4 (2004): 252, https://doi.org/10.1080/01674820400024406.

5. Rennie Negron, Anika Martin, Meital Almog, Amy Balbierz, and Elizabeth A. Howell, "Social Support During the Postpartum Period: Mothers' Views on Needs, Expectations, and Mobilization of Support," *Maternal and Child Health Journal* 17, no. 4 (May 2013): 621, https://doi.org/10.1007/s10995-012-1037-4.

6. H. Abigail Raikes and Ross A. Thompson, "Efficacy and social support as predictors of parenting stress among families in poverty," *Infant Mental Health Journal* 26, no. 3 (May/June 2005): 189, https://doi.org/10.1002/imhj.20044.

7. Rachel Zachariah, "Attachment, social support, life stress, and psychological well-being in pregnant low-income women: A pilot study," *Clinical Excellence for Nurse Practitioners* 8, no. 2 (June 2004): 60–67, https://www.researchgate.net/publication/287723318_Attachment_social_support_life_stress_and_psychological_well-being_in_pregnant_low-income_women_A_pilot_study.

8. Balaji et al., "Social Support Networks and Maternal Mental Health and Well-Being," 1388.

9. Robert S. Weiss, "The provisions of social relationships." In *Doing Unto Others* (Rubin Z., ed.), (Englewood Cliffs, NJ: Prentice-Hall, 1974), 18.

10. John Bowlby, *Maternal care and mental health*, (New York: Schocken Books, 1951), 11.

11. Diane Benoit, "Infant-parent attachment: Definitions, types, antecedents, measurement, and outcome," Paediatrics & Child Health, 9(8) (2004), 541, https://doi.org/10.1093/pch/9.8.541.

12. Van der Kolk, 113.

13. Neil W. Boris, Michael Fueyo, and Charles H. Zeanah, "The clinical assessment of attachment in children under five," *Journal of the American Academy of Child and Adolescent Psychiatry*, 36(2, February 1997), 291.

14. John Bowlby, *Attachment: Attachment and Loss Volume 1*, 2nd ed. (New York: Basic Books, 1983), 303.

15. Susan Kuchinskas, *The Chemistry of Connection: How the Oxytocin Response Can Help You Find Trust, Intimacy, and Love.* (Oakland, California: New Harbinger Publications, 2009), 6.

16. Amir Levine and Rachel S.F. Heller, *Attached: The New Science of Adult Attachment and How It Can Help You Find—and Keep—Love* (New York: Tarcher/Penguin Group, 2010), 8.

17. "Sex and intimacy after a baby," The Australian Parenting Website, Raising Children Network (Australia), last reviewed December 16, 2019, https://raisingchildren.net.au/grown-ups/looking-after-yourself/your-relationship/sex-intimacy-after-baby.

18. Scott I. Rick, Deborah A. Small, and Eli J. Finkel, "Fatal (Fiscal) Attraction: Spendthrifts and Tightwads in Marriage," *Journal of Marketing Research* 48, no. 2 (April 2011): 228, https://doi.org/10.1509/jmkr.48.2.228.

19. Dennis and Ross, "Women's perceptions of partner support and conflict in the development of postpartum depressive symptoms," 591.

CHAPTER 4—BUILDING YOUR CONFIDENCE: FROM "I CAN'T DO THIS" TO "I CAN DO HARD THINGS"

1. Jane Iles, Pauleen Slade, and Helen Spiby, "Posttraumatic stress symptoms and postpartum depression in couples after childbirth: The role of partner support and attachment. *Journal of Anxiety Disorders* 25, no. 4 (May 2011): 525, https://doi.org/10.1016/j.janxdis.2010.12.006.

2. "Infant Food and Feeding," American Academy of Pediatrics, accessed March 17, 2020, https://www.aap.org/en-us/advocacy-and-policy/aap-health-initiatives/HALF-Implementation-Guide/Age-Specific-Content/Pages/Infant-Food-and-Feeding.aspx.

3. "Infant Food and Feeding," American Academy of Pediatrics.

4. "Infant Sleep," Stanford Children's Health, accessed March 17, 2020, https://www.stanfordchildrens.org/en/topic/default?id=infant-sleep-90-P02237.

5. "Getting Your Baby to Sleep," The AAP Parenting Website, American Academy of Pediatrics, last modified July 16, 2018, https://www.healthychildren.org/English/ages-stages/baby/sleep/Pages/Getting-Your-Baby-to-Sleep.aspx.

6. Rebecca Felsenthal Stewart and Mary Ann LoFrumento, "Surviving Baby's First Cold," *Parents* (blog), June 11, 2015, https://www.parents.com/baby/health/sick-baby/babys-first-cold-flu-season/.

7. March of Dimes Perinatal Data Center, "Special care nursery admissions," PDF file, 2011. https://www.marchofdimes.org/peristats/pdfdocs/nicu_summary_final.pdf.

8. Juliana Menasce Horowitz, "Despite challenges at home and work, most working moms and dads say being employed is what's best for them," *Pew Research Center FactTank* (blog), September 12, 2019, https://www.pewresearch.org/fact-tank/2019/09/12/despite-challenges-at-home-and-work-most-working-moms-and-dads-say-being-employed-is-whats-best-for-them/.

9. Horowitz, "Despite challenges at home and work, most working moms and dads say being employed is what's best for them."

10. "Depression Among Women," Centers for Disease Control and Prevention.

11. Meyer, "Perinatal Mood Disorders: Overview."

12. Stone and Menken, 66.

13. "Perinatal Depression," National Institute of Mental Health, accessed March 17, 2020, https://www.nimh.nih.gov/health/publications/perinatal-depression/index.shtml.

14. Rada K. Dagher, Patricia M. McGovern, Bryan E. Dowd, and Ulf Lundberg, "Postpartum depressive symptoms and the combined load of paid and unpaid work: a longitudinal analysis," *International Archives of Occupational and Environmental Health* 84, no. 7 (October 2011): 739, https://doi.org/10.1007/s00420-011-0626-7.

15. "Anxiety During Pregnancy & Postpartum," Postpartum Support International, accessed March 19, 2020, https://www.postpartum.net/learn-more/anxiety-during-pregnancy-postpartum/.

16. "Any Anxiety Disorder," National Institute of Mental Health, last updated November 2017, https://www.nimh.nih.gov/health/statistics/any-anxiety-disorder.shtml.

17. Van der Kolk, 206.

18. "Postpartum Psychosis," Postpartum Support International, accessed March 19, 2020, https://www.postpartum.net/learn-more/postpartum-psychosis/.

19. Ana Fonseca and Maria Cristina Canavarro, "Exploring the paths between dysfunctional attitudes towards motherhood and postpartum depressive symptoms: The moderating role of self-compassion," *Clinical Psychology & Psychotherapy* 25, no. 1 (January/February 2008): e104, https://doi.org/10.1002/cpp.2145.

20. Kristin Neff, "Self-Compassion: An Alternative Conceptualization of a Healthy Attitude Toward Oneself," *Self and Identity* 2, no. 2 (2003): 88, https://doi.org/10.1080/15298860309032.

CHAPTER 5—RELEASING YOUR FEAR: FROM "I'M SCARED" TO "I AM BRAVE AND CAPABLE"

1. John Mordechai Gottman, *What Predicts Divorce?: The Relationship Between Marital Processes and Marital Outcomes* (Hillsdale, New Jersey: Lawrence Erlbaum Associates, Inc., 1994), 183.

2. Barbara L. Fredrickson and Marcial F. Losada, "Positive Affect and the Complex Dynamics of Human Flourishing," *American Psychologist* 60, no. 7 (October 2005): 678, https://doi.apa.org/doiLanding?doi=10.1037%2F0003-066X.60.7.678.

3. Stephen Ray Flora, "Praise's Magic Reinforcement Ratio: Five to One Gets the Job Done," *The Behavior Analyst Today* 1, no. 4 (January 2000): 66, https://doi.apa.org/fulltext/2014-43420-004.pdf.

4. Mark D. Seery, E. Alison Holman, and Roxane Cohen Silver, "Whatever does not kill us: Cumulative lifetime adversity, vulnerability and resilience," *Journal of Personality and Social Psychology* 99, no. 6 (December 2010): 1039, https://doi.org/10.1037/a0021344.

5. Beverly Rossman, Michelle M. Greene, Amanda L. Kratovil, and Paula P. Meier, "Resilience in Mothers of Very-Low-Birth-Weight Infants Hospitalized in the NICU," *Journal of Obstetric, Gynecologic & Neonatal Nursing* 46, no. 3 (May/June 2017): 443, https://doi.org/10.1016/j.jogn.2016.11.016.

6. David Fletcher and Mustafa Sarkar, "Psychological resilience: A review and critique of definitions, concepts, and theory," *European Psychologist* 18, no. 1 (April 2013): 21, https://doi.org/10.1027/1016-9040/a000124.

7. Fletcher and Sarkar, "Psychological resilience: A review and critique of definitions, concepts, and theory," 21.

CHAPTER 6—RESCUING YOUR HOPE: FROM "I FEEL HOPELESS" TO "I AM HOPEFUL AND RESILIENT"

1. Tali Sharot, *The Influential Mind: What the Brain Reveals About Our Power to Change Others* (New York: Henry Holt and Company, 2017), 59.

2. Richard S. Lazarus, "Hope: An Emotion and a Vital Coping Resource Against Despair," *Social Research* 66, no. 2 (Summer 1999): 666, https://www.jstor.org/stable/40971343?seq=1.

3. Charles S. Carver and Michael F. Scheier, "Optimism, pessimism, and self-regulation," in *Optimism & pessimism: Implications for theory, research, and practice* (Chang, E.C., Ed., Ann Arbor: U Michigan, 2001), 31.

4. Martin E. P. Seligman, *Learned Optimism: How to Change Your Mind and Your Life* (New York: Random House Vintage Books, 2006), 15.

5. C.R. Snyder and Shane J. Lopez, *Handbook of Positive Psychology* (Oxford, England: Oxford University Press, 2002), 693.

6. Seligman, 53.

CHAPTER 7—OWNING YOUR STRENGTH: FROM "I AM WEAK" TO "I CAN SHARE MY STRENGTH WITH OTHERS"

1.   Ryszard Praszkier, "Empathy, mirror neurons, and SYNC," *Mind & Society 15*, no. 1 (June 2016): 13, https://doi.org/10.1007/s11299-014-0160-x.

2.   Karen E. Gerdes and Elizabeth Segal, "Importance of Empathy for Social Work Practice: Integrating New Science," *Social Work* 56, no. 2 (April 2011): 144, https://doi.org/10.1093/sw/56.2.141.

3.   Brené Brown, "Vulnerability, courage, shame, and empathy: The living brave course." Accessed November 5, 2018, https://www.pesi.com/store/detail/23914/vulnerability-courage-shame-and-empathy.

4.   Theresa Wiseman, "A concept analysis of empathy," *Journal of Advanced Nursing* 23, no. 6 (June 1996): 1165, https://doi.org/10.1046/j.1365-2648.1996.12213.x.

5.   Elizabeth A. Segal, "Social Empathy: A Model Built on Empathy, Contextual Understanding, and Social Responsibility That Promotes Social Justice," *Journal of Social Service Research* 37, no. 3 (April 2011): 275, https://doi.org/10.1080/01488376.2011.564040.

6.   Neff, "Self-Compassion: An Alternative Conceptualization of a Healthy Attitude Toward Oneself," 92.

7.   Garriy Shteynberg and Evan P. Apfelbaum, "The power of shared experience: Simultaneous observation with similar others facilitates social learning," *Social Psychology and Personality Science* 4, no. 6 (2013): 738, https://doi.org/10.1177/1948550613479807.

8.   Michael Tomasello, Malinda Carpenter, Josep Call, Tanya Behne, and Henrike Moll, "Understanding and sharing intentions: The origins of cultural cognition," *Behavioral and Brain Sciences* 28, no. 5 (2005): 680, https://doi.org/10.1017/S0140525X05000129.

9.   Kyle Benson, "Repair is the Secret Weapon of Emotionally Connected Couples," *The Gottman Institute* (blog), February 23, 2017, https://www.gottman.com/blog/repair-secret-weapon-emotionally-connected-couples/.

10. "Pregnancy-Related Deaths," Centers for Disease Control and Prevention, last modified February 26, 2019, https://www.cdc.gov/reproductivehealth/ maternalinfanthealth/pregnancy-relatedmortality.htm.

11. Alison Hermann, Elizabeth M Fitelson, and Veerle Bergink, "Meeting Maternal Mental Health Needs During the COVID-19 Pandemic," *JAMA Psychiatry*, published online July 15, 2020, https://doi.org/10.1001/jamapsychiatry.2020.1947.

12. Charlotte V. Farewell, Jennifer Jewell, Jessica Walls, and Jenn A. Leiferman, "A Mixed-Methods Pilot Study of Perinatal Risk and Resilience During COVID-19," *Journal of Primary Care & Community Health* 11, no. 1 (2020): 3, https://doi.org/10.1177/2150132720944074.

13. Sharon Salzberg, "A Guided Loving-Kindness Meditation with Sharon Salzberg," *Mindful* (blog), The Foundation for a Mindful Society, May 14, 2020, https://www.mindful.org/a-guided-loving-kindness-meditation-with-sharon-salzberg/.

INDEX

A

abilities, building, 114. *See also* strengths
acceptance, 8–10, 48, 80, 94–95, 154, 168
Adichie, Chimamanda Ngozi, 26
advice, interpretation of, 51–52
affirmations, 102–103, 110
age of first-time mothers, increase in, 25
alliance, 156
alone time, 28
American Academy of Pediatrics, 86, 87
American Journal of Orthopsychiatry, 53
anger, 48
anxiety
    calming, 103–104
    postpartum, 17–18, 37, 98, 99–100, 103–104
anxious attachment, 69–70
anxious-avoidant attachment, 69
appreciation, 32, 114
assertiveness, 90–91
attachment, 63–70, 157
avoidant attachment, 69, 71

B

baby
    being secure base for, 67
    cuddling with, 28
    engaging mindfully with, 72
    feeding, 86
    illness or medical issues of, 94–95
    perspective of, 63
    sleep and, 86–87
    taking care of, 84–89
baby blues, 17
baking, 28
bargaining, 48
bath/shower, 29
bipolar disorders, 101
birth
    changes due to, 15–16
    exploring story of, 22
body
    conscious gratitude toward, 18
    honoring changes in, 18–19
    moving, 28
    physical changes in, 15, 16–17
boundaries, 146–147
Brantley, Jeffrey, 89
BraveNewMom.org, 177
breastfeeding, 86
breath, connecting to, 168
breathing, deep, 24, 28, 49–50, 71, 80, 82, 95, 103–104
Brown, Brené, 76, 142

C

calming yourself, 49–50
challenges, facing, 81
communication
    assertive, 90–91
    hope and, 135
    nonviolent, 90
    with partner, 89–91
    watching your language, 153–159
community, embracing, 56–77
confidence, building, 78–106
cooking, 28
COVID-19 pandemic, 57, 160
Crisis Text Line, 177
cuddling with your baby, 28
cultural rituals, 29
curiosity, 154

D

dancing, 29
deep breathing, 24, 28, 49–50, 71, 80, 82, 95, 103–104
denial, 48
depression
    loss and, 48
    postpartum (PPD), 17–18, 26, 37, 98–99
dialectical behavior theory, 88
Dialectical Behavior Therapy Skills Workbook, The (McKay, Wood, and Brantley), 89
disorganized attachment, 69

197

ACKNOWLEDGMENTS

So much goes into writing a book that you don't know until you are deep into it (and can't get out). Thank you to Dara Beevas for explaining it all to me, piece by piece, without judgment and with such compassionate wisdom. I truly don't know how people do this without a Dara.

And for the other gifted women who helped me make this book dream a reality—Maureen, Sarah, Emily, and Cindy. Because of them, it is more beautiful than I ever could have hoped.

I have so much gratitude in my heart for the moms who allowed me to share their stories here. Our stories and our innermost feelings are treasures, and I do not take their care lightly.

I want to thank my family. My partner and kids have so much to teach me about being in the moment, patient, creative, extroverted, and fun. We are a bunch of strong-willed beings and we challenge, love, and support each other every single day. It is never boring.

Thanks to everyone who got excited about this book, often at the exact right time when I was losing steam and needed your energy.

We are all of us.

To all the moms,

in the middle of the night

and

To my babies,

who awakened a strength in me

I didn't know existed

ABOUT THE AUTHOR

Jessie Everts, PhD LMFT, (she/her) is a therapist, mom, yoga/mindfulness teacher, writer, and consultant. She uses mindfulness practices along with cognitive and acceptance therapies to work with women and LGBTQ+ individuals who might be struggling with anxiety, parenting, postpartum mental health, work-life balance, trauma, and life transitions. Dr. Everts is a Licensed Marriage and Family Therapist. She is passionate about bringing mental health knowledge and skills to people outside of the therapy office and helping moms feel great about the amazing hard work they do. She lives in Minnesota with her spouse and two strong-willed children.